The Mount Vernon Cookbook

Compiled by
The Founders, Washington Committee
for Historic Mount Vernon

Published by
The Mount Vernon Ladies' Association
of the Union
Mount Vernon, Virginia

ISBN 0-931917-13-1

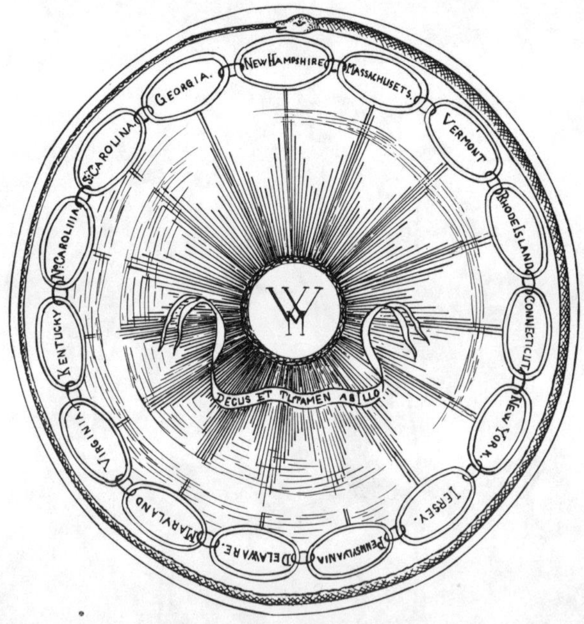

Plate from the "States service given to Mrs. Washington by "Mr. van Braam," a Dutchman and representative of the Dutch East Indian Company in 1796. The motto reads, " A glory and Defense from It."

First Printing, 1984
Second Printing, 1987
Third Printing, 1990
Fourth Printing, 1995

Contents

ACKNOWLEDGMENTS

The Founders Committee gratefully acknowledges all the friends of Mount Vernon across the country who generously shared their receipts with us. We regret that space limitations prevented the use of many splendid receipts. Those that were included were occasionally edited for uniformity.

The Founders also extend their warmest appreciation to the artist, Babs Gaillard; Charlotte Turgeon, professional consultant and friend of Mount Vernon; and Mrs. John P. Doyle, secretary to the Founders Committee. Special mention goes to those committee members who brought The Mount Vernon Cookbook to final completion: Mrs. A. Smith Bowman, Mrs. John Washington Davidge, Jr., Mrs. Donald D. Notman, Mrs. J. Woodward Redmond; and to Mrs. William Bradley Willard whose generous participation has played a large part in the enhancement of this publication.

The Mount Vernon Ladies' Association whose support made this cookbook possible should also be acknowledged. The editorial assistance of the Mount Vernon staff has been invaluable with special contributions from John Castellani, the Director; Christine Meadows, Karen Peters, and all members of the curatorial and library departments.

Proceeds from the sale of The Mount Vernon Cookbook will aid the Mount Vernon Ladies' Association in the preservation and maintenance of George Washington's home.

The Mount Vernon Cookbook

Founders, Washington Committee for Historic Mount Vernon 1984

Mrs. John W. Auchincloss
Mrs. A. Smith Bowman
Mrs. John W. Burke, Jr.
Mrs. Richard E. Byrd
Mrs. John Washington Davidge, Jr.
Mrs. John D. Firestone
Mrs. David duBose Gaillard, II
Mrs. Knight A. Kiplinger
Mrs. Juliette Clagett McLennan
Mrs. Thomas C. Musgrave
Mrs. Donald D. Notman
Mrs. Thomas A. Parrott
Mrs. J. Woodward Redmond
Mrs. William L. Ritchie
Mrs. Richard H. Streeter
Mrs. James W. Symington
Mrs. Timothy L. Towell
Mrs. William B. Willard

Mrs. Randall Hagner, Jr., *Chairman* and
Vice Regent for the District of Columbia

Cookbook Advisory Committee

Mrs. Harold A. Beatty
Mrs. A. Smith Bowman
Mrs. Richard E. Byrd
Mrs. John Washington Davidge, Jr.
Mrs. David duBose Gaillard, II
Mrs. Donald D. Notman
Mrs. C. Michael Price
Mrs. J. Woodward Redmond
Mrs. Henry Taft Snowdon
Mrs. Malcolm M.B. Sterrett

Mrs. Randall Hagner, Jr.

Martha Washington from the miniature painted by Charles Willson Peale in 1776.

Tea in the West Parlor

Julian Niemcewicz, a Polish visitor to Mount Vernon in 1798, related Martha Washington's memories of her youth when Englishmen would send a pound or two of tea to their colonial correspondents as a special favor. Here an original Pembroke table is set with Mrs. Washington's Chinese export tea service. Tea and coffee were generally served between 6 and 7 o'clock in the evening. During the cooler months or inclement weather, it would have been offered in the "Prussian blue" west parlor.

(Photograph by Paul Kennedy)

Introduction

In the years following the Revolution, George Washington's popularity brought a steady flow of visitors to Mount Vernon and his description of his home as a "well resorted tavern" carried more truth than exaggeration. Strange faces appeared routinely at the dinner table and dining alone was a privilege enjoyed by the Washingtons only twice in the last twenty years of their marriage. Born into a tradition of liberal hospitality, the Washingtons, like their Virginia neighbors, were accustomed to unexpected guests and dispensing a "bit of beef and toddy" to those who appeared at their door was part of plantation life. Those who stayed for long periods were treated like members of the household and their clothes, linens, horses and servants were all cared for by the Mount Vernon staff. Entertaining imposed heavy financial burdens and Washington complained in 1787 of exceedingly high expenses brought on "not from any extravagance, or an inclination on my part to live splendidly, but for the absolute support of my family and the visitors who are constantly here." Welcome as they were, the Washingtons' guests were expected to accommodate themselves to the family's domestic routine and those who expected constant attention or excessive entertainments were disappointed. Washington felt that his manner of living was "plain," but in fact he enjoyed a reputation among his contemporaries for keeping "an excellent table" and it was the opinion of one guest that his "entertainments were always conducted with the most regularity and in the genteelest manner...."

Household routines were firmly established with little variation from day to day. The hours for dining were set according to local custom and rigidly observed by the Washingtons. Attendance at table was not required, but those who elected to join the general company were expected to appear within five minutes of the dinner bell. General Washington's usual breakfast hour was seven in summer, and half past the hour in winter. Dinner was at three, and tea was served between six and seven o'clock. Supper, if offered, would have appeared about nine o'clock, but as this was Washington's usual hour for retiring, it was not part of the daily schedule. Supper is rarely mentioned in surviving accounts of visitors' experiences at Mount Vernon.

Meals might be served in any one of several mansion rooms depending on the size of the company and the season of the year. Guests could be served in their chambers, but most preferred to socialize with the family and other guests. Breakfast and dinner were regularly served in either of two dining rooms. A small one, situated off the first floor passage, accommodated no more than a dozen people comfortably. Before the completion of a large dining room on the north end of the mansion in 1787, overflow guests could be seated in the passage outside the small dining room which was set up with tables made from boards placed across saw horses and covered with tablecloths. This convenient arrangement was used later in the large dining room. Since the large dining room was used for other social gatherings, portable tables that could be enlarged or reduced in size were highly practical.

Guests who arrived between the regularly appointed hours for dining might be served in one of the parlors. One late arrival in 1798 was served breakfast in a small parlor overlooking the river. In an age when servants routinely moved chairs and small functional tables to suit any occasion, such accommodations were taken for granted. Tables were often carried into the passage for light refreshment or in good weather onto the piazza where Mrs. Washington presided at tea. This was the ideal setting in late afternoon when the sun had moved to the west and light southern breezes cooled the porch. In winter tea and coffee were brought to the parlors, which were warmed by open fires. Bell pulls were located in the mansion and on the piazza to summon the servants and the bells themselves were fixed on the south end of the mansion near the kitchen.

Mount Vernon was equipped with everything required for a genteel, well-appointed table. In general, Washington's table furnishings followed the current fashion, though economy was a necessary constraint and ostentation for its own sake was out of character for Washington. Before the Revolution he bought English goods, like other colonials, but after the war, he patronized American craftsmen and merchants whenever possible. English, French, and Chinese porcelains graced the Mount Vernon table. Blue and white china from Canton served for everyday use, but the Washingtons owned many sets of fine china. Examples of the china, silver and glassware used at Mount Vernon are exhibited in the museum there and are illustrated throughout this cookbook.

Table settings tended to follow the English custom where platters and serving dishes were symmetrically placed around the table. Contemporary English cookbooks offered helpful diagrams of proper table settings and evidence indicates that Mount Vernon adopted this traditional arrangement, though Martha Washington doubtless established certain procedures to suit her own taste and necessity. Her platters were garnished with vegetables or flowers and she followed the custom of offering a variety of foods from which the guests chose according to preference.

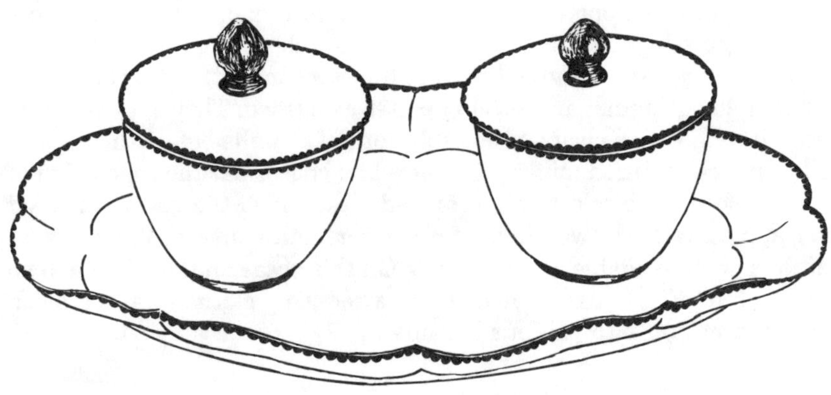

Sevres "confection" dish used to hold preserves for the dessert course.

Visitors' accounts provide good descriptions of the kinds of food and wine offered by the Washingtons. The master's usual breakfast was corn cakes "swimming in butter and honey," which he washed down with three cups of tea without cream. His guests, however, could choose from cold meats, bread, butter, coffee, tea or chocolate and an elaborate breakfast menu of 1802, "ham, cold corn-beef, cold fowl, red herring and cold mutton," would have satisfied the heartiest appetite. Ham was a Virginia staple and the ladies took great pride in the quality of their hams. Martha Washington cured her own and her grandson, George Washington Parke Custis, reported that one was boiled daily at Mount Vernon. At a time when any number of people might arrive unexpectedly for dinner, ham or a cold roast were useful and delicious provisions to have on hand.

Dinner, the principal meal of the day, consisted of soup, several kinds of fish, meat, vegetables and desserts or sweetmeats, as they were usually called. Amariah Frost, a guest in June, 1797, reported that he had "...a small roasted pigg, boiled leg of lamb, roasted fowels, beef, peas, lettice, cucumbers, artichokes, etc., puddings, tarts, etc., etc...." Winter menus offered many of the same meats and vegetables that carried through the cold months or were preserved in some way. Joshua Brookes, who visited the Washingtons in 1798, observed many details of service, the placement of dishes, and where each person sat. On the occasion of Brookes' visit, Mrs. Washington was at the head of the table and her husband to her right. Washington's secretary, Tobias Lear, was at the foot of the table. A leg of boiled pork was placed in front of Martha and a goose, before Lear. Roast beef, cold boiled beef, mutton chops and fried tripe completed the assortment of meats. Hommony, cabbage, potatoes, onions and pickles were also mentioned. The diners helped themselves and one another to the dishes before them which made for a busy and convivial scene. Three servants attended the guests and cleared the dinner and serving plates as needed. They kept the wine decanters filled and cleaned the tablecloth of crumbs before the dessert course which featured mince pies, tarts and cheese. At the conclusion of this course the tablecloth was removed after which the guests lingered over apples, raisins, two kinds of nuts, port and madeira. Wine, porter and beer were available during dinner. On this occasion the host gave no toasts, but Frost had noted that after the cloth was removed, Washington drank to "all our Friends."

This scene from the frieze of the marble mantelpiece in the Large Dining Room reflects Washington's keen interest in farming.

Numerous orders for madeira through the years establish it as one of Washington's favorite wines. Among original glassware now at Mount Vernon are six madeira glasses beautifully etched in a simple diamond pattern. His preference was a "rich oily Wine" which he expected his London agent to procure from the "best House in Madeira." In the hope of establishing a wine supply closer to home, Washington requested "a few setts or cuttings of the Madeira Grape (the kind...of which the Wine is made)" in 1768. Though nothing came of this, other attempts at viniculture were made later on.

In the course of serving a meal the servants traversed the distance between the mansion and the kitchen, which were connected by a colonnade, many times over. The kitchen was one of four outbuildings located on the Courtyard within the formal setting of the mansion. Architectural uniformity dictated that their appearance conform to the mansion's overall appearance and these buildings were finished like the mansion with beveled boards coated with sand to resemble stone. From the colonnade a door opened directly into the largest of three ground floor rooms where the principal fireplace was located. Here the cooks busied themselves roasting, stewing, boiling, frying and broiling the day's provisions. Multiple fires of different woods, depending on the type of heat desired, could be accommodated at the same time in a large fireplace. It was Mrs. Washington's habit before or after breakfast to go "through every household" department where the most important stop was the kitchen. Her grandson reported that she "...gave orders for dinner," at this time, "appointing certain provisions, a pr of ducks, a goose or a turkey to be laid by, and to be put down in case of the arrival of company; a very necessary provision in that hospital mansion...." The bread was prepared in the evening under her watchful eye; the dough rose slowly overnight in the warmth of the kitchen. Next morning it was baked in the beehive oven to the left of the fireplace. According to family tradition, there was no such thing as bad bread at Mount Vernon.

Mrs. Washington's morning inspection also included the larder and scullery. Perishables and other provisions were stored in the larder where the floor dropped three feet below ground level. A lattice located above the door admitted light and air. Within the larder a cool atmosphere helped preserve foods. Some dairy products were kept here but a spring house situated several hundred feet from the kitchen was the principal storage area for these products. The scullery, where a small fireplace could be used for auxiliary cooking, also provided storage space and a corner for washing dishes. From the scullery an enclosed staircase led to a half story above where two rooms provided quarters for a housekeeper.

A variety of equipment was available to the Mount Vernon cooks who usually numbered two. An inventory of the mansion and outbuildings prepared in 1799 following George Washington's death devotes three pages to the contents of the kitchen. Stew pans, platter covers, biscuit pans, an egg boiler, Dutch oven, cake pans, milk pans, "Chaffin Dishes," coffee pots, "Coffee Toasters," waffle irons, frying pans, trivets, skimmers, and cleavers are only a few of the nearly 200 utensils and pieces of equipment found there. The Mount Vernon kitchenware was carefully preserved by Martha Washington's descendants and several pieces may be seen today in the restored kitchen and museum on the estate.

Chinese export meat platter owned by Washington.

Also at Mount Vernon is Mrs. Washington's copy of *The Art of Cookery, Made Plain and Easy; Which far exceeds any Thing of the Kind yet published...By a Lady.* This popular cookbook first appeared in 1747 and went through many editions. Although the name Hannah Glasse was associated with the cookbook, it was thought to be a pseudonym for Dr. John Hill of London. Whoever the author, *The Art of Cookery* is a fascinating compendium of receipts of all kinds and also includes household hints, tips for marketing and a calendar of seasonal foods. Mrs. Washington probably owned a number of cookbooks, but her 1765 edition of *The Art of Cookery* and a manuscript cookbook in the Historical Society of Pennsylvania are the only ones known to survive. The latter under the title, *Martha Washington's Booke of Cookery,* was edited and annotated in 1981 by Karen Hess and was published by the Columbia University Press. It is a very early compilation of 16th and 17th century receipts and came into Martha's possession at the time of her marriage to Daniel Parke Custis who died in 1757.

No attempt has been made in *The Mount Vernon Cookbook* to transcribe the early receipts used by Mrs. Washington. Instead, the cookbook contains receipts having ingredients that were available to the 18th century cook but using modern methods of preparation and cooking. Many of the receipts have been handed down through many generations to the present contributors. It is hoped that those who peruse its pages and study the illustrations of original Mount Vernon objects will take pride and pleasure in the heritage of fine food and hospitality that characterized early America and most particularly the home of George and Martha Washington.

> *I can truly say I had rather be at Mount Vernon with a friend or two about me, than to be attended at the seat of government by the officers of State and the representatives of every power in Europe.*
>
> *George Washington to David Stuart, June 15, 1790*

Small Dining Room

The small dining room at Mount Vernon is painted, as it was in George Washington's lifetime, a vibrant vertigris green. Here, as was customary, the tablecloth was removed for a fruit, nut, and wine course that followed dessert. The 18th century glass "pyramid" on the table under the looking glass was a popular way to display "jellies" and sweetmeats.

(Photograph by Paul Kennedy)

Appetizers & Hors d'oeuvres

The colonnade served as a covered walkway for carrying food from the kitchen to the mansion.

APPLE HORS D'OEUVRES

Serves 8 to 10

2 firm, greenish, tart apples, peeled, cored and cut up
2 bunches spring onions
4 ounces cream cheese, softened
Lemon juice
Salt

Put apples and onions in food processor to grate. Add to cream cheese, stir in lemon juice and season with salt. Serve with crackers.

BOURBON CURRY SPREAD

¼ cup chutney, chopped
1 (8 ounce) package cream cheese
2 tablespoons Bourbon whiskey
½ to 1 teaspoon curry powder

Mix ingredients by hand or in blender. Fix in the morning and put in the refrigerator. Serve cold. Serve as a spread on your favorite crackers or small melba rounds.

CHEESE BISCUITS

Yield: About 36 biscuits

8 tablespoons butter
1 cup shredded sharp Cheddar cheese
1 cup unsifted flour
½ teaspoon dry mustard
Dash cayenne pepper
2 ounces Kellogg's® Rice Krispies

Preheat oven to 400 degrees. Mix butter and cheese. Put mustard and cayenne pepper in the cup of flour and add to the mixture. Mix until the mixture is the consistency of pie crust. Add the Rice Krispies and mix into dough. Make balls on an ungreased cookie sheet. Press with fork dipped in cold water. Bake for 10 minutes or more or until slightly brown. Cool on paper toweling. *This can be done by hand or in a food processor. In either case, add the Rice Krispies by hand.*

CHEESE BALLS

Yield: 20 balls

3 (3 ounce) packages cream cheese
4 teaspoons horseradish, drained
2 teaspoons mayonnaise, highly seasoned
1/8 teaspoon salt
1 teaspoon onion juice
1 teaspoon Worcestershire sauce
Minced parsley or paprika

Combine first 6 ingredients. Form into balls. Roll in minced parsley or paprika.

CHEESE FILLED CUMQUATS

Serves 10 to 15

½ pound fresh cumquats
1 pint water
¾ cup sugar
3 ounces cream cheese
Cream

Cook well-washed cumquats for 15 to 20 minutes; drain. Make a syrup of water and sugar. Boil 5 minutes. Add cumquats and boil slowly until liquid is syrupy and the fruit is transparent. When cool, drain and cut in half. Scoop out the interior and stuff the halves with cream cheese blended with a little cream to make it smooth.

DEVILED CHEESE BALLS

1 (8 ounce) package cream cheese
1 (4½ ounce) can deviled ham
½ cup blue cheese
Chopped nuts or chopped parsley

Mix first 3 ingredients thoroughly. Roll into 1 large or about 45 small balls. Roll in chopped nuts or chopped parsley. Serve the large ball with crackers. The small balls are sufficient unto themselves.

CHICKEN LIVER PÂTÉ EN GELÉE

Serves 30

2 pounds chicken livers
½ pound lean country-type sausage
1 small onion, chopped
½ teaspoon ginger
¼ teaspoon cinnamon
¼ teaspoon cloves
1 tablespoon Worcestershire sauce
3 tablespoons cognac
8 tablespoons butter, melted

Sauté chicken livers, sausage and onion over very low heat for approximately 45 minutes. Drain off fat. Cool slightly and process in food processor or blender with the seasonings and melted butter. Chill for several hours in a 1-quart mold, tightly packed.

Aspic
2 cups chicken broth, homemade or canned
1 tablespoon gelatin
2 tablespoons sherry
Finely chopped parsley

Soften gelatin in ½ cup of the broth. Heat the rest of the broth and dissolve gelatin in it. Add sherry. Chill until it starts to jell, stirring frequently. Unmold the pâté on a serving plate and coat the pâté with a thin layer of aspic. Chill until layer has jelled and repeat process until aspic coating is of desired thickness. To serve, garnish with chopped parsley. Serve with homemade melba toast. *If desired, the pâté may be frozen for 2 weeks before the aspic is added. The aspic can be made and the pâté en gelée completed the day before it is to be served.*

DIFFERENT CONSOMMÉ MOUSSE

Serves 8

2 (10½ ounce) cans consommé
12 ounces cream cheese
1 to 2 tablespoons curry powder to taste
1 (3½ ounce) jar lumpfish roe
½ cup minced chives

Blend together in processor until smooth the consommé, softened cream cheese, and curry powder. Pour into individual ramekins and refrigerate covered with plastic wrap. Just before serving, garnish with roe and/or chives.

EGG AND CAVIAR MOUSSE

Serves 10

1 (2 ounce) jar caviar (Beluga, golden or lumpfish)
1 tablespoon gelatin
¼ cup water
6 hard-boiled eggs, chopped
½ cup mayonnaise
½ cup sour cream
Salt and pepper to taste
1 teaspoon Worcestershire sauce
Juice of ½ lemon
1 tablespoon grated onion
Toast rounds
Watercress

Dissolve gelatin in cold water and put container in hot water over low heat to melt gelatin. Mix the eggs, mayonnaise, sour cream, salt and pepper, Worcestershire sauce, lemon juice and grated onion. Then add gelatin and caviar. Divide mixture between 10 individual molds or put in a small decorative mold. Refrigerate until set. To serve, put toast rounds on individual plates, unmold molded mousse on top and garnish with watercress. Or serve the single mold on a platter surrounded by melba squares for a cocktail spread.

ELIZABETH'S HORS D'OEUVRES

Serves 6

6 (2½-inch to 3-inch) bread rounds, lightly toasted
6 slices tomato
1 pound backfin crabmeat
1 cup mayonnaise
1 bunch watercress
1 egg, hard-boiled
1 lemon

Place toast rounds on platter or individually on plates. Add to each, 1 slice of tomato, portion of crabmeat that has been gone through lightly for shell and dollop of mayonnaise lightly colored with cocktail sauce. Grate egg and sprinkle on top. Surround with generous amount of crisp watercress. Serve with a lemon wedge on side.

MUSHROOMS GREEK STYLE

Serves 12 or more

3 pounds mushrooms, trimmed, washed and sliced
⅓ cup olive oil
Juice of 1 lemon
2 large onions, sliced
2 cloves garlic, crushed
½ teaspoon thyme
½ teaspoon marjoram
½ teaspoon pepper
3 bay leaves
3 cups canned plum tomatoes, drained and chopped
¼ cup red wine vinegar or other flavored vinegar
1 teaspoon sugar
Dash hot pepper sauce
2 to 3 tablespoons minced parsley (optional)

In large skillet sauté the sliced mushrooms until golden in 2 tablespoons olive oil. Do this in 2 batches if necessary. Transfer mushrooms to large bowl and toss with the lemon juice. In same skillet sauté the onions and garlic with the remaining olive oil until onions are softened but not browned. Add thyme, marjoram, pepper and bay leaves and sauté 1 minute. Stir in the canned tomatoes, vinegar, sugar and hot pepper sauce and simmer 20 minutes. Add mixture to the mushrooms and salt to taste. Cool, cover and marinate at least 12 hours or up to 3 days in the refrigerator. Sprinkle with parsley. Serve at room temperature with thin sliced rye or pumpernickel bread which has been buttered and sprinkled with minced parsley. *This can be served as a cocktail hors d'oeuvre or as a first course. It will serve 12 people for the latter and many more at cocktail time.*

MUSHROOM SNACKS

Yield: 24 snacks

24 bread rounds
Butter
1 pound mushrooms, chopped
Salt and pepper to taste
6 tablespoons chopped parsley
Cream

Sauté bread rounds in butter until golden on both sides. Sauté chopped mushrooms in butter with salt, pepper and 5 tablespoons of parsley until tender. Mix mushrooms with enough cream to make a paste. (The mixture must not be drippy, so you might need to drain mushrooms before adding cream.) Spread on toast rounds and sprinkle with remaining parsley. Serve hot or cold.

TIDEWATER MUSHROOMS

1 pound medium-large fresh mushrooms
1 pint oysters (medium size)
Salt and pepper
Melted butter
White wine or sherry

Remove stems from mushrooms; wipe clean. Drain oysters and pat dry with toweling. Dip mushrooms in melted butter and place cup side up on a well-greased shallow pan. Put an oyster in each cup, sprinkle with salt and pepper, dot with butter and ½ teaspoon white wine or sherry. Broil under moderate heat until edges of oysters curl. Serve around a dish with cocktail sauce and horseradish for those who wish it.

ONION PUFFS

Serves 18

1 cup mayonnaise
2 small spring onions, finely diced
Parmesan cheese
12 slices firm white bread, cut into small squares

Preheat oven to 350 degrees. Combine mayonnaise and onion and add enough cheese to make the consistency of whipped cream. Spread thickly on bread and bake in the oven about 15 minutes or until light brown.

GRILLED OYSTER HORS D'OEUVRES

Serves 12 to 16

48 oysters
Flour
Cooking oil

Dredge oysters in flour. Grill on lightly-buttered grill or blazer over fire until brown. Turn only once. Sprinkle with cooking oil. When done, serve with sauce made by combining and heating the sauce ingredients.

Sauce
3 tablespoons melted butter
⅓ cup lemon juice
1 cup A-1 Sauce
⅓ cup Worcestershire sauce
¾ cup sherry or madeira

Keep the sauce hot and well blended. Serve the oysters on toothpicks, from the blazer, dipped in the sauce.

HOT PEANUT BUTTER CANAPÉS

20 melba toast rounds
Peanut butter (crunchy or smooth)
Chutney, chopped
5 slices crisp bacon, crumbled

Spread melba toast rounds with peanut butter. Top with chutney. Sprinkle crisp bacon, finely crumbled, on top. Heat in 350 degree oven until peanut butter and chutney spread is hot. Serve immediately.

BAKED POTATO SKINS

Serves 4 to 6

6 large baking potatoes
Olive oil
Butter
Salt
Pepper
Garlic powder (optional)
Parmesan cheese (optional)

Preheat oven to 425 degrees. Scrub potatoes and then grease them lightly with olive oil. Pierce them with a fork. Bake for 1 hour. Cool. Cut potatoes in half lengthwise and scoop out the meat, leaving ¼-inch to ⅛-inch shell. Reserve meat for another meal. Reduce oven temperature to 325 degrees. Place potato skins in oven-proof dish or baking pan. Bake skins for an additional 10 to 20 minutes. Spread butter on inside of skins, sprinkle with salt, pepper, garlic powder and Parmesan cheese, if desired. Bake 10 to 15 minutes more until crisp. Serve hot.

ROQUEFORT CANAPÉS

Yield: As many as you like

Sweet butter
Roquefort cheese
Brandy to taste (optional)

Mix equal parts of sweet butter and roquefort cheese. Brandy to taste, optional. Spread between 2 halves of walnuts or in raw mushroom caps.

The Dove of Peace weathervane was made in Philadelphia by Joseph Rakestraw and was placed on top of the cupola in the fall of 1787.

SUSAN'S SPINACH DIP

Serves 10 to 12

1 package frozen chopped spinach, cooked and drained
1 cup mayonnaise
1 cup sour cream
1 tablespoon dried Italian salad dressing mix
½ teaspoon dill weed
¼ cup chopped green onions
¼ cup parsley flakes
Juice of ½ lemon

Cook spinach according to directions on package. Drain well, pressing out all excess water. Mix all ingredients together. Refrigerate covered. Will keep in refrigerator for about 6 weeks. Serve in a small bowl surrounded by your favorite crackers.

SHRIMP-ARTICHOKE HORS D'OEUVRES

Serves 10

10 large shrimp, cooked
¼ cup mayonnaise
3 shakes TABASCO brand pepper sauce
1 teaspoon onion juice
Salt and pepper to taste
Cream (measured to spreading consistency)
Paprika
Artichoke bottoms (canned or packed in jars)

Place shrimp, mayonnaise, TABASCO, onion juice, salt and pepper in blender. Add cream until spreading consistency. Place dollop in artichoke bottoms and add sprinkle of paprika to each. Allow 2 per person.

RAW VEGETABLE DIP

Serves 10 to 15

1 (3 ounce) package cream cheese
1 tablespoon Bovril (beef extract)
1 small onion
½ jar Roquefort cheese spread
2 cups mayonnaise

Blend the cheese and Bovril. Cut the onion in half and scrape with a sharp knife to give you 1 to 1½ teaspoons of onion juice. Combine with cheese and mayonnaise. Serve with thin slices of zucchini, strips of green pepper, celery, cauliflower, carrot, etc.

JALAPEÑO PEPPERS AND CHEESE

Yield: Approximately 60 squares

6 eggs
1 pound sharp cheese, shredded
3 or 4 chopped jalapeño peppers, or to taste

Preheat oven to 350 degrees. Beat eggs. Add cheese. Butter a 9-inch pyrex dish and spread chopped peppers on bottom. Add cheese and egg mixture. Bake in oven until done (approximately 30 minutes). Cut in small cubes to serve.

SHARP CHEDDAR LACE COOKIES

Yield: As many as you like

Place small dabs of sharp Cheddar cheese on a cookie sheet lined with parchment paper and bake in 375 degree oven for approximately 15 minutes.

VIRGINIA HAM BISCUITS

Yield: About 40

2 cups all-purpose flour
2 teaspoons double-acting baking powder
½ teaspoon salt
¼ cup cold lard
1 cup milk
Unsalted butter, for spreading on biscuits
80 very thin slices Virginia ham (about 1 inch in diameter)
Baking sheet, buttered

Preheat oven to 450 degrees. In a bowl, sift together the flour, baking powder and salt. Blend in the lard, cut into bits, until the mixture resembles coarse meal. Stir in ¾ cup milk, or enough to make a soft dough. Form the dough into a ball and roll or pat it out ½ inch thick on a floured surface. Cut out rounds with a 1-inch cutter dipped in flour and transfer them to a baking sheet. Form the scraps gently into a ball, roll and cut the dough in the same manner and transfer the rounds to the baking sheet. Brush the tops of the rounds lightly with milk and bake the biscuits in the middle of the oven for 10 to 12 minutes or until they are puffed and golden. Let the biscuits cool on the racks, split them, and if desired spread them with unsalted butter. Put 2 very thin slices of ham on ½ of each biscuit. Reform the biscuits and serve them as hors d'oeuvres.

COCKTAIL SAUSAGES

1 pound small link sausages
½ cup dark brown sugar
½ cup soy sauce
½ cup dark rum

Cut the sausages into ⅓'s and brown them in a skillet over moderate heat, turning as necessary. In a shallow heat-proof serving dish, heat the sugar and soy sauce, stirring until the sugar dissolves. Add the rum and stir in the sausage. Remove from the heat. Cool. Cover and refrigerate 24 hours. Reheat before serving. Leftover sauce can be refrigerated and used again.

SEA ISLAND SHRIMP

Serves 8 to 12

1 bay leaf
⅛ teaspoon cayenne pepper
½ cup sugar
½ teaspoon fresh ground pepper
2 cups tomato juice (you may substitute vegetable juice)
1 cup vinegar
1 large onion, thinly sliced
1 tablespoon (or more) chopped fresh parsley
1 tablespoon salt
Juice 2 lemons
¼ cup catsup
24 medium to large shrimp, cooked and shelled
1 lemon, sliced

In a large bowl or plastic container, mix all ingredients except shrimp and lemon together well. Add shrimp; stir and mix to coat them well. Marinate 2 to 6 hours in refrigerator. To serve, remove from refrigerator ½ hour before serving. Stir well and either pour marinade and shrimp into non-metal serving bowl or serve from bowl in which it rested. Add thinly-sliced lemon on top and sprinkle with more fresh parsley if you wish. Use a long-handled spoon to remove shrimp onto plate or to be "stabbed" with toothpicks. It is nice to have melba toast or crackers next to shrimp bowl in case guests would like to put the shrimp on top. More or less of most ingredients does not matter. Add extra tomato juice for more liquid if it doesn't appear to be juicy enough. For large numbers of shrimp, make 2 batches and as you remove shrimp from 1 serving bowl, add shrimp to marinade in kitchen.

Soups

Food brought from the kitchen was prepared for serving in the "sweetmeat closet." Soup tureens are pictured on the top shelf.

COLD AVOCADO SOUP

Serves 6 to 8

- 2 ripe avocados
- ½ cup plain yoghurt
- 3 cups chicken broth (preferably homemade)
- 1 tablespoon lemon juice or more, to taste
- Curry powder (optional)
- Salt and pepper to taste
- ¼ cup minced green onions, including green part
- 2 large tomatoes, peeled, seeded and chopped coarsely
- 2 or 3 tablespoons crisp and crumbled bacon (optional)

Put peeled, cut-up avocados in blender or food processor with yoghurt, broth, lemon juice, optional curry powder, salt and pepper. Process until very smooth. Chill, tightly covered. The plastic wrap cover should touch the top of the soup to keep it from turning brown. Garnish each serving with onion, tomatoes and optional bacon, or they may be stirred in before serving. *If you cannot find good, ripe fresh tomatoes, use canned tomato wedges or sliced tiny tomatoes.*

BROCCOLI SOUP

Serves 4

- 2 cups milk
- 2 tablespoons flour
- 2 tablespoons butter
- 1 teaspoon salt
- Dash white pepper
- ½ teaspoon ACCENT® Flavor Enhancer
- 1 cup cooked chopped broccoli (fresh or frozen)
- 4 sprigs parsley
- ½ cup celery leaves
- 1 medium onion, sliced thin
- Paprika for garnish

Combine all ingredients in food processor or blender except paprika. When well blended, heat in double boiler 15 to 20 minutes, stirring occasionally. Ladle soup into cups and sprinkle with paprika.

ENGLISH BEEF SOUP

Serves 5 to 6

1 pound top round of beef
6 cups cold water
2 teaspoons salt
¼ cup fine barley
¼ cup green split peas
8 peppercorns
2 medium onions, chopped
½ cup chopped carrots
½ cup chopped celery
2 tablespoons chopped parsley

Combine cold water, top round cut in small pieces and salt in a 4-quart soup pot. Bring to a boil slowly, skim thoroughly and add barley, split peas and peppercorns. Cover and simmer gently for 1½ hours. Add chopped onions, carrots and celery and simmer ½ hour longer, stirring frequently. To serve, sprinkle with chopped parsley. *Storing overnight in the refrigerator improves flavor.*

BLACK BEAN SOUP

Serves 8 to 10

1 pound best quality black beans
1 pound lean veal
1 ham bone
1 lemon, cut into 8 pieces
3 cloves, stuck in the lemon pieces
¼ teaspoon allspice
¼ teaspoon pepper
2 tablespoons Worcestershire sauce
2 tablespoons butter
3 onions, chopped
1 cup sherry
Salt to taste

Wash thoroughly and soak black beans overnight. Drain. In a large soup kettle, combine beans, 2 quarts of fresh water, the veal and bone, lemon pieces, dry seasonings and Worcestershire sauce. Bring to a boil and reduce heat. Cook slowly until beans are mushy, about 3 to 4 hours. Add more water if thinner consistency is desired. Remove meat, shred and set aside. Remove lemon and cloves and discard. Press beans through a sieve and add the meat. In butter fry the onions until brown and add to the soup. Add sherry and more salt or pepper, if desired. Heat to boiling point. Garnish each serving with a slice of hard-boiled egg.

CANTALOUPE SOUP

Serves 4 to 6

1 (2 pound) cantaloupe
2½ cups water
⅔ cup superfine sugar
1 cup dry white wine
Lemon juice
1 cup sour cream

Scoop the flesh from the cantaloupe. Dissolve sugar in water over low heat, then simmer for 5 minutes. Cool the syrup. Purée the cantaloupe with the wine in a blender or food processor. Add the cooled syrup gradually. Add some lemon juice to sharpen the taste and 1 cup sour cream. Serve chilled and garnish with mint leaves. *When preparing fruit, always use stainless steel utensils.*

CHICKEN ALMOND CURRY SOUP

Serves 4

1½ tablespoons butter
1 tablespoon curry powder
1 tablespoon flour
3 cups chicken broth
4 egg yolks
1 cup cream
1 cup chopped almonds
Minced parsley

Melt butter; smooth in curry powder and flour. Add chicken stock. Cook 10 minutes in double boiler. Beat egg yolks. Add cream. Combine with chicken broth. Cook over hot, not boiling, water. Chill until very cold. Add chopped almonds and serve, garnished with minced parsley.

QUICK CHICKEN CURRY SOUP

Serves 6

1 can cream of chicken soup
1 can cream of celery soup
1 small can applesauce
1 tablespoon curry powder
1 cup half and half
Chopped chives

Put all ingredients in blender until thoroughly mixed. Pour into cups and sprinkle with chives. Can be served hot or cold.

SENEGALESE

(COLD CURRIED CREAM OF CHICKEN SOUP)

Serves 8

2 tablespoons finely diced onion
2 tablespoons butter
2 teaspoons curry powder
1 tablespoon flour
3½ cups chicken stock
4 egg yolks
2 cups heavy cream
¼ cup finely diced chicken meat
1 red apple, cored and diced

Sauté onion in butter until soft, not brown. Add curry powder, flour and cook slowly 5 minutes. Add stock and bring to a boil, stirring until smooth. Whip egg yolks until light yellow, then whip in and cook 1 minute more. Cool. Add cream and chicken. Blend 1 minute in blender. Serve very cold with apple croutons.

CLAM CHOWDER ALIBI

Serves 24

1 gallon shucked clams
1 pound butter
1 bunch leeks, white part only
4 quarts half and half
1 gallon milk
1 pound bacon, cooked very crisp and dry and broken into small pieces
1 quart bottled clam juice
5 pounds potatoes, boiled
2 small envelopes mashed potato mix
Parsley

Drain salty juice from clams and set aside. (Use only a small amount of this clam juice to season.) Sauté the clams in ½ pound of butter. Mince the clams in a food processor or blender. Slice white part of leeks, sauté in ½ pound of butter with a little clam juice and run through the blender. In a large pot combine clams, half and half, milk, sautéed leeks, crisp chopped bacon, diced cooked potatoes and chopped parsley. Thicken with potato mix. Serve in a large tureen sprinkled with chopped parsley.

HEARTY CORN CHOWDER

Serves 6 to 8

4 strips bacon, cooked and crumbled
¼ cup chopped green pepper
½ cup chopped onion
⅓ cup butter or margarine
2 tablespoons flour
½ teaspoon salt
¼ teaspoon seasoned pepper
1 teaspoon parsley flakes
½ bay leaf
¼ teaspoon poultry seasoning
4 cups milk
2 (1 pound, 10 ounce) cans cream-style corn
2 cups cooked, cubed potatoes

Drain crisp fried bacon on absorbent paper. Sauté green pepper and onion in butter until tender. Blend in flour and seasonings. Gradually add milk, corn and cubed potatoes. Cook over medium heat until thick and creamy, stirring occasionally. Just before serving, stir in crumbled bacon, saving some to sprinkle on top.

CARROT VICHYSOISSE

Serves 4 to 6

2 cups peeled and diced potatoes
1¼ cups sliced carrots
1 leek (white part only), trimmed, washed and sliced
3 cups chicken stock
1 teaspoon salt
1 cup cream
1½ teaspoons chives, chopped

Simmer potatoes, carrots and leek in the chicken stock for 25 minutes or until tender. Purée the vegetables in a food mill or blender. Empty into bowl or pitcher and stir in salt and cream. Chill. Serve very cold in individual soup cups or bowls. Top with chopped chives.

The Larder

The kitchen larder was used for storing leftovers and other perishables for short periods of time. Built about 3½ feet below floor level, the larder is naturally several degrees cooler than the kitchen itself. A lattice-work grill over the door permits air to circulate freely and also allows warm air to escape from the room, further cooling it. George Washington was especially fond of pineapples, admitting in a diary entry for December 22, 1751, that no fruit *pleases my taste as do's the Pine[apple].*

(Photograph by Paul Kennedy)

CARROT ZUCCHINI SOUP

Serves 6

4 tablespoons margarine
2 medium onions, chopped
2 cups grated carrots
2 small zucchini, grated
4 tablespoons flour
5 cups chicken broth
Salt
Pepper
¾ cup milk

In soup pot melt margarine and sauté onions and carrots together. Cook for 5 to 7 minutes, stirring frequently. Then add the zucchini which has been pressed to remove excess water. Cook and stir another 5 minutes. Sprinkle the flour on top of the mixture and mix well. Add the broth, salt and pepper. Simmer for 30 minutes and just before serving add the milk. Serve hot or cold.

CRAB BISQUE

Serves 6 to 8

1 (10½ ounce) can tomato soup
1 (10½ ounce) can green pea soup
20 ounces (or 1 carton) half and half
1 can (or 6½ ounces) crabmeat, flaked
½ cup sherry

Mix tomato soup and green pea soup. Add the half and half gradually, stirring between additions to remove any lumps. Add the crabmeat and heat. Add ½ cup sherry at the last minute. *A dollop of unsweetened whipped cream added to each bowl before serving makes a nice presentation.*

SIMEON'S COLD CRAB SOUP

Serves 5 to 6

1 quart buttermilk
1 cup fresh lump crabmeat
1 teaspoon salt
1 level teaspoon sugar
1 cup peeled, diced cucumber
1 tablespoon dry mustard
1½ tablespoons fresh dill or 2 teaspoons dry dill

Mix all ingredients and chill for as long as possible before serving. Serve with a thin slice of cucumber, not peeled, on top with a sprinkling of paprika.

CUCUMBER YOGHURT SOUP FOR SUMMER

Serves 4

2 large cucumbers
1 clove garlic
1 tablespoon lemon juice
1 to 2 tablespoons chopped dill
1 pint plain yoghurt
1 tablespoon chopped mint
Salt and pepper to taste

Peel and remove most of the seeds from cucumbers. Process all ingredients in blender or food processor briefly until cucumber is finely chopped. It should retain a slightly crunchy texture. Chill well. May be made a day or 2 ahead. For a change, add a 6-ounce can of tomato juice.

FISH CHOWDER

Serves 8

½ pound salt pork, diced
3 medium onions, sliced
5 medium potatoes, cubed
2 pounds filet of haddock, skinned
1 quart milk (approximately)
1 small can evaporated milk
Butter

Fry salt pork until crisp. Leave 4 or 5 pieces of pork and 1 tablespoon of fat in pot. Dispose of remaining fat and drain pork on paper towels. Simmer 3 slices of onion in fat. Add remaining onions, cover with water and boil for 5 minutes. Add potatoes and more water to cover. Simmer until nearly cooked. Lay haddock, cut in large pieces, on top of potatoes and onions and simmer until cooked. Add enough milk to cover haddock. Add evaporated milk. Heat but do not boil. Before serving, add salt and pepper to taste, sprinkle with pork bits and dot with a bit of butter. Some like to add a dash of Worcestershire or A-1 sauce. This is usually served with pilot biscuits.

GAZPACHO

Serves 8 to 10

½ cup olive oil
4 tablespoons lemon juice
6 cups tomato juice
2 cups beef broth
½ cup finely minced onions
2 tomatoes, cubed
2 cups finely minced celery
⅛ teaspoon TABASCO brand pepper sauce
2 teaspoons salt
¼ teaspoon fresh black pepper
2 green peppers, chopped
2 cucumbers, chopped
Diced croutons

Beat together the oil and lemon juice. Stir in the tomato juice, broth, onions, tomatoes, celery, Tabasco, salt and pepper. Taste for seasonings. Chill for three hours. Put in a tureen. Serve green peppers, cucumbers and croutons separately in small bowls.

SAN ANTONIO GUMBO

Serves 12 to 18

15 tablespoons bacon drippings
18 tablespoons all-purpose flour
6 onions, chopped fine
4½ cups finely chopped celery
3 cloves garlic, minced
3 (1 pound, 12 ounce) cans tomatoes
3 cans tomato sauce
3 packages frozen cut okra
15 to 18 cups water
3 tablespoons salt
1 pound German sausage
½ pound ham, diced
6 pounds shrimp, shelled and deveined
1 tablespoon gumbo filé
9 tablespoons Worcestershire sauce
1 tablespoon chili powder
1 pint oysters

Make a roux of the bacon drippings and the flour, browning well. Add onions and celery and cook until transparent. Add minced garlic, tomatoes, tomato sauce, okra, and 15 or more cups of water, along with 3 tablespoons of salt. Cook for 2 to 3 hours on low heat. Add diced sausage and diced ham and cook for 1 hour. Add shrimp and cook 10 minutes. Add gumbo filé, Worcestershire sauce, chili powder. Add oysters if you do not plan to freeze. The gumbo will be thick. Serve over rice.

PURÉE OF JERUSALEM ARTICHOKE SOUP

Yield: 6 large plates or 12 small cups

5 cups (approximately 2 pounds) Jerusalem artichokes (also called sunchokes in California)
¼ celery root (celeriac)
2 cups water
1 teaspoon salt
6 cups clear veal stock or chicken broth
1½ tablespoons butter
3 tablespoons flour
Salt
White pepper
Pinch of sugar, to taste
2 or 3 egg yolks
⅓ cup heavy cream

Wash and scrape artichokes (preferably under running water). Rinse and place for 1 hour in about 6 cups of water, to which has been added 2 tablespoons each vinegar and flour to prevent darkening. Peel celery root and cut into small cubes. Add to artichokes. Drain. Reserve 12 small artichokes and cook in small amount of the stock. Place remainder in 2 cups cold water with 1 teaspoon salt. Bring to boil and cook until quite soft. Purée in blender or food processor. Heat butter with 3 tablespoons flour, stirring. Cook for 2 minutes. Add purée and veal stock and cook 5 more minutes. Add salt, white pepper and pinch of sugar, to taste. Whisk egg yolks and heavy cream in tureen or large bowl. Pour in soup. Decorate plates with reserved whole artichokes.

Chinese export "blue and white" soup tureen.

MAUD'S CREAM OF MUSHROOM SOUP

Serves 6

4 celery tops with leaves
2½ cups chicken broth (fresh or canned)
1½ pounds fresh mushrooms
4 tablespoons butter
½ teaspoon salt
¼ teaspoon white pepper
3 teaspoons cornstarch
⅓ cup milk
2 cups light cream

Combine celery and chicken broth in saucepan. Bring almost to boiling point. Lower heat; cover and simmer 15 minutes. After washing, sauté mushrooms lightly in butter and chop in blender with strained broth, salt and pepper. Place mixture in heavy saucepan over low heat until hot but not boiling. To thicken, mix until smooth cornstarch, milk and cream and add slowly to above mixture.

JELLIED MUSHROOM SOUP

Serves 6 to 8

1 pound mushrooms, chopped
3½ cups strong chicken stock
2 tablespoons dry sherry
Salt and pepper to taste
1 to 2 tablespoons lemon juice
¼ cup cold water
1 envelope unflavored gelatin
Sour cream
Watercress, parsley or chives

Simmer mushrooms in stock for 3 minutes. Place in blender for 30 seconds. Add additional stock if necessary to make 3¾ cups. Add sherry, salt, pepper and lemon juice. Soften gelatin in cold water. Bring soup to boiling point, add gelatin and stir until dissolved. Chill. Serve with dollop of sour cream and snipped watercress, parsley or chives.

CURRIED FRESH PEA SOUP

Serves 10

3 tablespoons butter
3 tablespoons flour
5 cups strong, well-seasoned chicken broth
3 cups puréed peas (fresh or frozen)
1 cup cream (half and half)
1 tablespoon curry powder
Salt and pepper to taste
1 tart apple

Heat the butter and stir in the flour. Simmer 3 minutes. Slowly add chicken stock and cook until thickened. Add puréed peas and cream; add seasoning. Chill 4 hours. Should have the consistency of heavy cream. Must be served very cold! Peel apple, slice finely and cut into julienne strips. Add just before serving so apple will not discolor.

BUTTERNUT SQUASH SOUP

Serves 8

1 butternut squash
1 onion
1 green pepper
2 tomatoes, peeled
1 clove garlic
2 carrots, peeled
2 stalks celery
1 cup cream
1 cup milk
1 cup chicken stock
1 teaspoon salt
2 dashes hot pepper sauce
1½ teaspoons curry powder
Sour cream

Wash and boil squash in salted water until soft. Drain. Cut up, peel and remove seeds. Boil onion, green pepper, tomatoes, garlic and celery in salted water until soft. Remove celery. Put squash and vegetables in a big bowl. Purée squash, vegetables, cream, milk and chicken stock in blender. Add hot sauce, curry powder and salt. If too thick, add more cream or milk. Serve cold with a spoonful of sour cream.

YELLOW SQUASH SOUP

Serves 8 to 9

3 tablespoons butter
3 large onions, chopped
2 or 3 cloves garlic, minced or pressed
2 pounds yellow summer squash
½ teaspoon sugar
3 cans chicken broth
2 cups buttermilk or yoghurt or 1 cup sour cream plus 1 cup yoghurt
Salt
White pepper
Fresh basil

Sauté the onions and garlic in butter without browning. When tender, add the squash cut into slices. Then add chicken broth and cook until squash is tender. Add the sugar. For last few minutes add a fistful of basil from which you have saved enough for sprinkling on top of each bowl of cold soup. When the mixture is cooked and cooled, drain the liquid from the squash and reserve. Put squash through blender with 2 cups of either the buttermilk-yoghurt mixture or the sour cream-yoghurt mixture. Combine squash mixture with reserved cooking liquid and blend well. Refrigerate. Before serving, season to taste. Serve in cold bowls, garnished with chopped basil.

SUMMER PEACH SOUP

Serves 4

4 ripe peaches
2 cups dry white wine
1 cup water
3 tablespoons sugar
¼ teaspoon cinnamon
¼ teaspoon curry powder
3 cloves
1 orange, thinly sliced (for garnish)

Place peaches in boiling water for 1 minute. Peel, halve, stone and purée in blender. Transfer to a pan and add remaining ingredients. Bring to a boil; simmer 10 minutes. Let soup cool. Chill. Garnish with thinly sliced orange.

ZUCCHINI SOUP

Serves 10 to 12

8 tablespoons butter
1 medium onion, sliced
1 clove garlic, minced
3 pounds zucchini, trimmed, washed and sliced
2½ cups rich chicken broth
1½ cups heavy cream
½ tablespoon curry powder
Salt and pepper
Sour cream

In a saucepan over medium heat, heat butter. Sauté onion, garlic and squash until soft and golden. Purée the mixture in a processor or by hand. Return to pan and add broth, cream, curry and salt and pepper. Cook on low heat 15 minutes to blend flavors. Serve hot or cold. Garnish with a spoonful of sour cream.

WATERCRESS SOUP

Serves 4

2 tablespoons butter
1 small onion, chopped
1 bunch watercress, chopped
4 cups chicken bouillon
1 medium potato, boiled
Salt and pepper to taste

Heat butter in large saucepan and sauté onions until soft, 3 to 4 minutes. Add watercress and sauté for 2 minutes. Add bouillon, bring to a boil and simmer for 10 minutes. Pour mixture into blender and add boiled potato. Blend until smooth. Season to taste.

FRESH TOMATO SOUP

Serves 4 to 6

6 tomatoes, peeled, seeded and chopped into small pieces
2 cups tomato juice
1 bunch green onions, finely minced
1 tablespoon minced fresh basil or 1½ teaspoons dried basil
1 tablespoon finely chopped fresh tarragon or oregano or 1½ teaspoons dried tarragon or oregano
4 tablespoons light olive oil
Salt
Pepper

Place first 6 ingredients in large bowl. Toss gently with oil. Season with freshly ground pepper and a little salt. Chill. Serve with crusty rolls.

CHILLED TOMATO ÉMINCÉ SOUP

Serves 6

7 large ripe tomatoes
1 medium onion
1½ teaspoons salt
¼ teaspoon black pepper
5 teaspoons mayonnaise
1¼ teaspoons curry powder
2 teaspoons chopped parsley

Scald and peel the tomatoes. Place in a large bowl and mince very finely or use a food processor, exerting care not to reduce the mixture to a pulp. Grate the onion and add to the tomatoes. Add salt and pepper to taste. Chill. Serve in crystal soup bowls with a sauce of the mayonnaise and curry powder mixed together with parsley sprinkled on top.

TOMATO BISQUE

Serves 4 to 6

4 tablespoons unsalted butter
1 medium onion, minced
2 tablespoons flour
2 pounds fresh tomatoes or 2 (14½ ounce) cans pear-shaped tomatoes
½ teaspoon thyme
½ teaspoon basil
2 cups chicken broth

Melt the butter in a heavy saucepan. Sauté the onion until translucent, about 10 minutes. Stir in the flour and continue cooking for 3 minutes. Peel the tomatoes; core, seed and juice them. After coring, squeeze firmly over sink, removing any remaining seeds with your fingers. For canned tomatoes, do not use the liquid they are packed in. Chop the tomatoes finely. Add the tomatoes, herbs and chicken broth to the onions and simmer 20 minutes. Season to taste. Run ½ of the soup through a food mill, mix together and ladle into soup bowls.

SUSIE'S SORRELL SOUP

Serves 4

2 tablespoons butter
3 sprigs parsley
1 pint sorrell, chopped
1 red onion
2 tablespoons flour
2 cups strong chicken stock
4 egg yolks
1 cup sour cream
Pinch each nutmeg, salt and pepper

Melt butter in skillet. Chop parsley, sorrell and onion fine. Cook in melted butter until tender. Add flour, then stock. Simmer for 10 minutes. Beat 4 egg yolks and add to mixture. Add sour cream, salt, pepper and nutmeg. Taste and correct for seasoning. Do not boil after adding sour cream.

WINTER VEGETABLE SOUP

Serves 6

2 leeks
2 turnips
1 medium size celery root
2 tablespoons butter
1 large onion, chopped
2 large potatoes
2 cups chicken broth
Salt
Pepper
1 cup rich milk
5 ounces shredded soft mild cheese (Port Salut or American)

Trim and wash leeks, turnips and celery root. Dice thin. Crop the onions and slice. Lightly brown the onions in a 2-quart saucepan in 2 tablespoons of melted butter. Add the diced vegetables, cover tightly and simmer for 20 minutes. Peel and wash the potatoes. Add to the saucepan, sliced thinly, with 2 cups of chicken broth. Salt and pepper to taste. Bring to a boil and simmer for 45 minutes. Add milk and cook 15 more minutes. Mix in a blender and serve piping hot in a soup tureen with the shredded cheese on top, which should melt into the soup. Serve with croutons, chives or minced bacon on top.

Seafood

The Washington family often had tea and punch on the piazza in good weather. From a watercolor by Benjamin Latrobe in 1796.

STUFFED CATFISH

Serves 8

4 pound catfish
1 pound cooked crayfish or shrimp

Broil a 4-pound catfish for 20 minutes or bake in a 350 degree oven for 20 minutes. Cut off head and tail (save) and remove large bone in center.

Stuffing

4 ounces butter or margarine
½ cup green pepper
½ cup green onion
¼ cup celery leaves
1 cup seasoned bread stuffing
¼ teaspoon cayenne pepper
½ teaspoon black pepper
2 teaspoons salt

Sauté the above ingredients in butter or margarine and when softened add 1 pound of cooked crayfish or shrimp. Stuff the fish with this mixture and replace head and tail. Pour ¼ pound of melted butter or margarine over fish and reheat. Add fluted lemon and parsley for decoration.

CLAMS SOUTHSIDE

Serves 24

1 gallon shucked clams
1 pound butter
1 quart bottled clam juice
¾ cup flour
1 pint heavy cream

Drain salty juices off clams, set aside. Sauté clams in ½ pound butter. Mince clams in food processor or blender. Add bottle of clam juice. Add very small amount of other clam juice, enough to season. Heat the remaining butter in a large saucepan. Whisk in the flour and cook very gently for 3 minutes. Do not brown. Add the cream and whisk until smooth. Stir the clams and juices into sauce. Serve hot on toast.

CLAM FRITTERS

Serves 6 to 8

24 cherrystone clams (or other medium-sized hard-shelled clams)
2 cups flour
½ cup milk
2 eggs
2 teaspoons double-acting baking powder
½ teaspoon salt
¼ teaspoon pepper
Oil for deep-fat frying

Clean and shuck the clams, reserving the liquor, and mince them. In a bowl stir together the flour, milk, eggs, baking powder, salt and pepper until the mixture is combined. Stir in the reserved liquor, a little at a time, add the clams and combine the batter well. In a deep fryer drop the batter by tablespoons into hot deep oil (375 degrees) and fry the fritters, turning them for 2 minutes or until they are golden. Transfer the fritters with a slotted spoon to paper towels to drain and sprinkle them with salt.

DEVILED CRAB

Serves 6

1 pound fresh lump crabmeat
1 large egg
2 tablespoons Dijon mustard
1 tablespoon Worcestershire sauce
½ teaspoon salt
¼ teaspoon cayenne pepper
¼ teaspoon black pepper
2 tablespoons grated fresh onion
2 tablespoons cream or mayonnaise
1 to 2 tablespoons bourbon whiskey
1 cup fresh bread crumbs
¼ cup melted butter
½ cup chopped parsley

Pick over crabmeat and put in large bowl. Boil egg 2 minutes until fully firm but still soft enough to mash. With hand beater or broad-tined fork, mash egg with mustard, Worcestershire sauce, pepper, salt and onion. Add to crabmeat. Add cream or mayonnaise. Add whiskey to taste. Fill shallow shells or ramekins with mixture. Top with buttered bread crumbs. Bake at 375 degrees for 20 minutes. Sprinkle each dish with chopped parsley. *This is good as a first course alone or as a main course served with rice, sweet slaw and stewed tomatoes.*

CRABMEAT REMICK

Yield: 4 large or 6 small servings

1 pound lump crabmeat
2 tablespoons butter or margarine
4 strips bacon, cooked and crumbled
1 scant teaspoon dry mustard
½ teaspoon celery salt
Few drops TABASCO brand pepper sauce
½ cup chili sauce
1 teaspoon tarragon vinegar
¾ cup mayonnaise

Sauté lump crabmeat in butter. Place in individual shells or ramekins. Crumble 1 strip of crisp bacon into each shell. Blend together dry mustard, celery salt and Tabasco sauce. Add chili sauce and tarragon vinegar. Mix well and add mayonnaise. Spread the warmed crabmeat with this sauce and glaze under the broiler.

CHARLESTON MEETING STREET CRAB

Serves 4 generously

1 pound white crabmeat
4 tablespoons butter
4 tablespoons flour
½ pint whipping cream
Salt and pepper to taste
4 tablespoons Madeira
¾ cup sharp cheese, shredded

Pick over crabmeat to remove shell. Heat the butter and whisk in the flour. Cook slowly for 2 to 3 minutes without browning. Whisk in the cream and continue whisking until smooth. Add salt, pepper and Madeira. Remove from fire and add crabmeat. Pour mixture into buttered casserole or individual baking dishes. Sprinkle with shredded cheese and cook in hot oven (400 degrees) just until cheese melts. Do not overcook.

ELEGANT CRAB CASSEROLE

Serves 8 to 9

2 pounds backfin crabmeat
2 eggs
¼ teaspoon dry mustard
Salt and white pepper
2¼ cups mayonnaise
4 tablespoons chopped pimento (optional)
¼ cup Parmesan cheese

Pick over crabmeat to remove any shell or filaments. Beat eggs in a large mixing bowl with mustard, salt and pepper. Combine mayonnaise with mixture and blend gently. Fold in pimentos and crabmeat. Pour into an ungreased 2-quart casserole. Sprinkle cheese on top. Bake at 350 degrees for 20 minutes or until slightly brown and bubbly.

SOUFFLÉ DE CRABE

Serves 10

6 small crabs or 2 cartons of crabmeat
8 tablespoons (½ cup) Bechamel sauce, fairly thick
8 tablespoons (½ cup) tomato purée
8 tablespoons (½ cup) fresh cream
3 tablespoons fresh white bread crumbs
4 tablespoons boiled rice
3 tablespoons finely chopped onions
3 coffee spoons curry powder
A little butter
Salt, pepper, paprika and cayenne to taste
3 egg yolks
3 egg whites, beaten to a peak

Cook minced onions in a little butter for 1 minute, add the crabmeat, the cream, the Bechamel sauce, the rice, the breadcrumbs and the spices. Bring the mixture to a boil, then add the tomatoes and the 3 egg yolks, stirring briskly. Remove from fire, let it cool a little and fold in the stiffly beaten egg whites. Pour into an oven-proof soufflé dish that has been well-greased with butter. Put a buttered band of paper around top of dish. Put the soufflé dish in a bain marie in a hot oven (400 degrees) for 30 minutes. *This delicate soufflé cannot possibly wait for late gourmets, so have the gourmets sit down and, if necessary, wait for it.*

BAKED FISH FLORENTINE

Serves 4

4 fish filets (any fine-grained white fish such as flounder, fluke or lemon sole)
1 package frozen spinach, thawed
¼ pound fresh mushrooms
1 cup mayonnaise
1 cup plain yoghurt
2 to 3 tablespoons lemon juice
Salt and pepper to taste
1 ounce butter

Cut mushrooms that have been trimmed and briefly rinsed into ½-inch pieces and sauté quickly in butter until they give up their liquid. Squeeze liquid completely from spinach. Mix mayonnaise, yoghurt, lemon juice, salt and pepper. Mix together about one-fourth of the mayonnaise mixture with the spinach and mushrooms. Roll each filet around several tablespoonfuls of the spinach mixture. Place filets in a shallow baking dish with any extra spinach mixture and cover with the rest of the mayonnaise mixture. Bake at 350 degrees for 20 to 30 minutes until fish flakes. Alternative: Use 1 big piece of fish for 4 people. Place it on a bed of the spinach mixture in a baking dish, cover with the sauce and bake the same time as the filets. *It is possible to prepare spinach, mushrooms and sauce early in the day and assemble shortly before cooking.*

GRILLED FLOUNDER PICANTE

Serves 4 to 6

½ cup butter, melted
¼ cup lemon juice
½ teaspoon marjoram
¼ teaspoon dry mustard
1 teaspoon salt
White pepper
2 tablespoons chopped parsley
2 pound fresh flounder filets, skinned

Combine all ingredients except flounder and marinate flounder in this mixture for 2 hours. Place flounder inside a fish grilling rack and cook over hot coals for approximately 5 minutes on 1 side and 7 minutes on the other side. Baste fish with marinade while it is cooking. *A hinged grilling rack is essential so that the fish can be easily turned.*

LOBSTER, SHRIMP AND CRABMEAT CASSEROLE

Serves 6

1 pound boiled lobster meat
1 pound shelled, cooked shrimp
1 pound crabmeat or 2 (½ pound) cans crabmeat
1 pound mushrooms
½ cup Parmesan cheese, grated
½ cup fine bread crumbs
1 tablespoon butter
1 cup dry white wine
4 tablespoons finely chopped parsley
2 tablespoons finely chopped green or white onion
2 cups cream sauce

Sauté mushrooms in butter. Add to cooked shellfish. Mix bread crumbs and cheese (for topping). Put wine, parsley and onions in pan and boil to reduce to about 3 tablespoons. Strain. Add to white sauce. Mix ¾ of this sauce with the fish and mushrooms, pouring into buttered casserole and topping with rest of the sauce and cheese/bread crumb mixture. Bake at 350 degrees for 30 minutes. Watch to make sure the top does not burn. Place a few shrimp on the top for the last 15 minutes of cooking. To do ahead heat *without* bread crumbs for 20 minutes and then add crumbs and a little melted butter and cook for 20 minutes more or until very hot.

LOBSTER NEWBURG

Serves 2 to 4

The meat from 2 cooked lobsters (approximately 1¼ pounds), cut up
6 tablespoons butter
Salt and cayenne pepper
¼ cup sherry or Madeira
2 egg yolks, slightly beaten
1 cup heavy cream

Sauté the lobster meat quickly in the butter. Add seasoning and wine. Mix the egg yolks with the cream and pour over the lobster. Cook in double boiler until slightly thickened, as with custard. Serve with rice or toast points.

MUSSELS MADEIRA WITH LINGUINI

Serves 8

12 pounds fresh mussels, scrubbed, debearded and steamed; save broth
1 small onion, chopped fine
3 cloves garlic, chopped fine
¼ pound butter, melted
8 tablespoons flour
1½ cups milk
1½ cups cream
1 cup broth from mussels
Salt and pepper to taste
¼ cup Madeira wine
½ cup chopped parsley
1 (16 ounce) package linguini
1 tablespoon salt
2 tablespoons olive oil
Parsley sprig for garnish

Shell mussels, discarding any unopened. Remove black rims; reserve. Place onion and garlic with butter in a 12-inch skillet and sauté for about 5 minutes. Strain and place butter sauce in skillet. Off heat, add flour and stir until smooth. Transfer to 2-quart top of double boiler. Gradually stir in milk and cream to make a white sauce; stir until thickened and smooth. Place over hot water. Add mussels, salt, pepper, Madeira wine and parsley. Keep hot. Break linguini strands in 3 parts and place in a large 8-quart pot in boiling, salted water and the olive oil. Stir and boil for about 6 to 8 minutes. Test. Drain linguini in large colander and return to pot. Serve at once with linguini in the center of a heated platter with the mussel sauce surrounding it. *The mussel sauce may be made the day before serving. If the sauce thickens too much, thin with more mussel broth before serving.*

DAVID'S ESCALLOPED OYSTERS

Serves 4 to 6

1 quart oysters

Place oysters and liquor in pan and heat for about 5 minutes or until the liquor just comes to a boil. Drain and save liquor (do not let liquor boil). Make medium white sauce.

White Sauce
2 tablespoons butter
2 tablespoons flour
½ cup warm cream
¾ of the oyster liquor
Salt and pepper to taste
Dash Worcestershire sauce

Melt butter in saucepan and add flour. Stir until absorbed. Add cream and oyster liquor, stirring constantly until thickened. Season with salt, pepper and Worcestershire sauce. Place oysters in buttered casserole and pour sauce over them. (Sauce should be medium thickness.) Use your judgment of how much sauce you pour over oysters. Cover with bread crumbs and layer if desired.

Buttered Crumbs
Bread, crusts removed
1 tablespoon soft butter

Chop fine *fresh* bread with crusts removed, add 1 tablespoon of soft butter and mix with fingers lightly. Place in oven (350 degrees) and cook for 15 minutes or until crumbs are golden brown.

EASY SCALLOPED OYSTERS

Serves 6

1 quart standard oysters
1 package saltine crackers
Salt and pepper to taste
Butter
Milk or light cream
Worcestershire sauce, optional

In shallow buttered baking dish, place a layer of oysters, then a layer of crumbed crackers. Season with salt and pepper and dot with butter. Sprinkle with Worcestershire. Repeat, making 2 layers. Pour in enough milk or cream to nearly cover oysters. Cook at 350 degrees until oysters curl at the edges and most of the liquid is absorbed (25 to 30 minutes).

NEW ORLEANS OYSTER GUMBO

Serves 8

3 tablespoons margarine or bacon fat
3 tablespoons flour
4 cups sliced okra
1 cup finely chopped onion
1 cup chopped green onion tops and celery leaves
1 cup finely chopped celery
1 cup chopped red or green bell pepper
2 cloves garlic, minced
3 quarts chicken stock
Salt
Red pepper or TABASCO brand pepper sauce
1 quart oysters
1 tablespoon Chinese oyster sauce (available in Oriental food stores)
2 tablespoons gumbo filé
2 tablespoons chopped parsley
Boiled rice

Melt fat and mix in flour. Stir until it turns into a dark brown roux. This takes about 15 minutes. Add okra, onion, green onion and celery tops, celery, peppers and garlic. Cook, stirring frequently, for about ½ hour until okra is very tender, adding a bit of stock if necessary. Heat chicken stock and stir into vegetable mixture and simmer 15 to 20 minutes. Season to taste with salt, TABASCO or red pepper. Add oysters, their liquor, and Chinese oyster sauce and simmer for about 10 minutes. Ladle into tureen or soup bowls and sprinkle each serving with gumbo filé and parsley. Place a large spoonful of rice in each bowl.

OYSTERS AND BACON

Serves 4

1 pint oysters, fresh
Herb seasoned stuffing mix
6 strips bacon
Parsley, chopped coarsely

Preheat oven to 400 degrees. Place drained oysters in scallop shells (for individual servings) or in a shallow casserole. Cover with seasoned stuffing mix. Cut bacon into 1-inch pieces and cook until barely crisp. Place on top of stuffing or several pieces to each individual shell. Sprinkle chopped parsley on top. Bake for 15 to 20 minutes or until bacon is crisp.

SALMON MOUSSE

Serves 6

1 (15½ ounce) can top-grade salmon
1 cup mayonnaise
8 ounces whipped cream cheese
10 ounces tomato juice
¾ cup finely chopped celery
1½ tablespoons finely grated onion
1½ packages gelatin

Remove skin and any bone from salmon and reserve ½ cup juice. Gently flake the meat with a fork. Heat tomato juice and dissolve cheese into this. Dissolve gelatin in salmon juice and add to the tomato juice and cheese. Set mixture aside and when cool, combine with salmon, celery and onion. Fold in mayonnaise and mix well. Place in 1-quart fish mold that has been rinsed with cold water. Refrigerate 3 to 4 hours. Unmold on platter and decorate with slices of hard-boiled egg, watercress and capers.

SEAFOOD GUMBO

Serves 12 to 16

1 gallon homemade chicken stock or canned broth
1 pound okra, trimmed and sliced
4 tablespoons butter
2 cloves garlic, minced
2 medium-sized onions, minced
1 green pepper, minced
2 ribs celery, minced
1 (16 ounce) can tomatoes, chopped
1 (8 ounce) can tomato sauce
1 to 2 tablespoons Worcestershire sauce
½ teaspoon salt
½ teaspoon sugar
Prepared seafood seasoning to taste, approximately 1 teaspoon
½ gallon oysters
5 pounds shrimp, cleaned
3 pounds crab claws
6 cups rice

Prepare the stock. Sauté okra in 2 tablespoons of butter separately until dry, stirring frequently. Add to chicken stock. Then sauté garlic, onions, green pepper and celery together until vegetables are tender and add to stock. Add tomatoes, tomato sauce, Worcestershire sauce, salt, sugar and seafood seasoning to stock. Simmer 1 hour. Cool and refrigerate. The gumbo is better made a day ahead. Skim the gumbo before reheating. Before serving, add oysters, shrimp and crab claws to the gumbo. You may add seafood according to the number of people to be served. Cook seafood until just done. Avoid overcooking. Serve as an entrée in soup bowls on a mound of rice.

BANTRY BAY SCALLOPS

Serves 4

1 pint bay scallops
2 tablespoons butter or margarine
1 tablespoon brandy, warmed
1 tablespoon lemon juice
½ teaspoon salt
⅛ teaspoon pepper
Dash cayenne pepper
¼ cup light cream

Sauté scallops in butter for 3 minutes. Add brandy. Ignite. Sprinkle with lemon juice, salt, pepper and cayenne. Add cream; heat but do not boil. Serve in individual casseroles along with toast points.

SCALLOP CASSEROLE

Serves 3 to 4

1 pint bay or ocean scallops, cut in fourths
½ cup melted butter
1 cup cracker crumbs
¾ cup light cream
1 tablespoon sherry
Salt and pepper to taste

Preheat oven to 400 degrees. Butter a casserole dish (9x9-inch). Place in it a layer of scallops, then crumbs, then scallops, then crumbs. Salt and pepper the scallops lightly as you put them in. *No more than 2 layers.* Pour in cream and sherry. Bake uncovered for 25 minutes.

SEAFOOD CASSEROLE

Serves 6

1 cup shrimp, cooked and cleaned
1 cup crabmeat
4 tablespoons chopped onion
1 cup chopped celery
½ cup mayonnaise
½ teaspoon dry mustard
½ teaspoon Worcestershire sauce
Salt and pepper to taste
Buttered bread crumbs

Preheat oven to 350 degrees. Cut shrimp in half and mix with crabmeat. Add all ingredients except bread crumbs. Mix lightly and put in greased casserole. Top with buttered bread crumbs and cook until crumbs are lightly browned.

MR. JEFFERSON'S SHAD

Serves 6 to 8

2 shad filets, totaling 1½ pounds
1 pair shad roe, about 10 to 12 ounces
1 tablespoon vinegar
1 teaspoon salt
1 bay leaf
3 sprigs parsley
¼ cup butter
1 onion, finely minced
¼ cup flour
1 cup milk
1 cup chopped parsley
¼ cup white wine
3 eggs
1 lemon
Butter
Paprika

Preheat oven to 375 degrees. Butter a baking dish large enough to hold the shad in a single layer. Prick the roe with a needle and parboil in water to cover with vinegar, salt, bay leaf and parsley for about 10 minutes or until firm. Drain, cool and remove membrane. Melt the butter in a saucepan and add the onion. Cook over low heat until the onion is soft but not brown. Add roe, breaking gently with fork. Cook until roe eggs are separated and covered with butter. Add flour and stir until blended. Add milk and cook until thick, stirring gently. Add chopped parsley and white wine. Remove from heat. Separate the egg whites from the yolks. Gradually add the yolks, slightly beaten, with the juice of 1 lemon. Salt to taste. Stir until well blended. Gently fold in stiffly beaten egg whites. Spread roe mixture over shad, dot with butter and sprinkle with paprika. Bake for 20 minutes.

...I have cured a sufficient quantity of fish for our people, together with about 160 or 70 barrels of shad for the Continent...

Lund Washington to George Washington,
May 6, 1778

BAKED SHAD

Serves 4 to 6

2¼ pound shad

Split shad. Place skin side down in pan. Cook 15 minutes per pound (35 minutes total for 2¼ pound shad) in 375 degree oven, basting with sauce every 5 minutes.

Sauce

10 tablespoons Worcestershire sauce
¼ pound butter, melted
½ tablespoon salt
½ tablespoon black pepper
¼ teaspoon dry mustard
½ tablespoon vinegar
Juice of ½ large lemon

Mix Worcestershire sauce, melted butter, salt, pepper, mustard, vinegar and lemon juice. Heat and use to baste shad.

BROILED SHRIMP WITH GARLIC

Serves 6

2 pounds jumbo shrimp
¼ cup flour
¼ cup olive oil
¼ cup melted butter
2 tablespoons minced garlic
4 tablespoons minced parsley
1 cup drawn butter sauce

Shell shrimp and leave tails on. Dry; dust with flour. Mix oil and butter in flat baking dish. Add shrimp and broil under medium heat for 8 minutes. Make drawn butter sauce.

Drawn Butter Sauce

4 tablespoons butter
2 tablespoons flour
1 teaspoon lemon juice
Freshly ground black pepper
1 cup hot water

Melt 2 tablespoons of butter, add flour, lemon juice and pepper and stir until smooth. Add cup of hot water and bring mixture to a boil, stirring constantly. Reduce heat and cook 5 minutes. Add remaining 2 tablespoons of butter and stir until melted. Add the garlic and parsley to this sauce. Pour sauce over the shrimp and stir to coat all shrimp. Broil for 2 minutes and serve immediately.

BARBECUED SHRIMP

Serves 4

1½ sticks butter
Juice 2 lemons
¼ cup peppercorns
2 tablespoons paprika
2 tablespoons Worcestershire sauce
3 pounds large whole shrimp, peeled

Melt butter in iron skillet. Add lemon juice, peppercorns, paprika, Worcestershire sauce and shrimp. Cook 2 minutes on each side and serve with sauce from pan.

CURRIED SHRIMP

Serves 8

3 pounds medium-sized shrimp
4 tablespoons (½ stick) butter
1 medium onion, chopped
1 level tablespoon hot Madras curry powder
3 level tablespoons flour
1 quart half and half
1 level teaspoon salt
1 level teaspoon sugar
1 teaspoon Worcestershire sauce
1 tablespoon lemon juice
1 dash TABASCO sauce
1 dash angostura bitters
1 pinch nutmeg

Bring 2 quarts of salted water to a rolling boil. Drop in the shrimp; boil for 2 minutes after the water begins to boil again. When the shrimp are cool, peel and devein them. In a large, heavy, covered saucepan, sauté chopped onion in the butter until it is soft and a golden color. Add the curry powder and flour. Carefully stir in the half and half to make a smooth sauce. Transfer the sauce to a large double boiler. Add the remaining seasonings and then add the shrimp. Serve with steamed rice and as many of the following condiments as you wish: Chutney, shredded coconut, ground peanuts, chopped bacon, chopped hard-boiled egg. Chutney is the essential accompaniment.

BROILED SHRIMP ESPAGNOL

Serves 6

3 pounds shrimp
1½ cups olive oil
5 garlic cloves, crushed
2 tablespoons chopped mint
2½ teaspoons chili powder
1 tablespoon ground turmeric
1 tablespoon basil
2 tablespoons vinegar
1 teaspoon salt
Freshly ground black pepper

Shell and wash shrimp. Marinate in remaining ingredients for at least 6 hours. Pour shrimp and marinade into shallow pan and broil under high heat 6 to 10 minutes, turning once. Serve with the marinade. *Langostinos are also good prepared this way.*

SHRIMP CASSEROLE

Serves 4

6 tablespoons butter
1½ cloves garlic, minced
6 teaspoons chopped parsley
3 large tomatoes, peeled, halved and seeded
6 tablespoons flour
3 cups heavy cream
1 tablespoon sherry
3 tablespoons Worcestershire sauce
3 drops angostura bitters
4 cups shrimp (2 pounds raw shrimp)
Bread crumbs
Parsley

Preheat oven to 350 degrees. In a sauté pan melt butter and cook the garlic, parsley and tomato until soft. Add flour and cook 2 more minutes. Add cream, sherry, Worcestershire, bitters and heat 5 minutes longer. Put the shrimp in a 3-quart buttered casserole and pour sauce over it. Sprinkle with bread crumbs and bake 25 minutes. Garnish with parsley.

GRILLED SWORDFISH STEAK

Swordfish steak
1 small can V-8 juice
1 small can grapefruit juice
Juice of ½ lemon or to taste
Small amount oil
Basil or oregano to taste

Marinate fish in above ingredients in refrigerator for 4 hours or more. Broil or barbecue on a grill for 5 minutes on each side.

FILET OF SOLE MONICA

Serves 6

2 pounds filet of sole or flounder
1 cup milk
½ teaspoon salt
1 pound mushrooms
2 tablespoons butter
¾ pound seedless grapes
4 tablespoons butter
4 tablespoons flour
1 cup Cheddar cheese, shredded
½ cup whipping cream
Salt and pepper to taste
Paprika

Simmer fish in the milk with salt added until firm. Remove with spatula and save the milk. Briefly rinse the unpeeled mushrooms and cut in medium sized pieces. Cook in 2 tablespoons of butter. Halve the grapes. Heat the butter and whisk in flour. Add milk and any mushroom juice and shredded cheese. Stir over medium heat until smooth. Add cream. Season to taste. Pour some sauce in bottom of 1½-quart pyrex dish or casserole and alternate layers of fish, grapes, mushrooms and sauce, finishing with sauce. Put a little paprika on top. Bake 20 minutes at 400 degrees. Be careful not to bake too long as grapes will thin out the sauce. *This can be made in the morning and baked just before serving.*

EASY FILET OF SOLE

Serves 4

1 onion
4 small tomatoes, cored
3 tablespoons butter
Salt and pepper to taste
8 small pieces flounder, sole or white fish
½ pint sour cream

Slice onion very thin. Slice tomatoes in half. Melt butter in a flat baking dish and sauté onion until transparent. Cook tomato halves separately in a frying pan for 3 to 4 minutes. Then spread tomatoes on top of onions. Salt and pepper fish on both sides and place on top of tomatoes. Broil, dotted with butter, a few minutes until cooked through and brown on top. Cover with sour cream and broil again until sour cream turns brown in patches.

FILET OF SOLE AMANDINE, BAKED IN CREAM

Serves 4

6 filets of sole
Juice of 1 lemon
1 cup chopped mushrooms
¼ cup minced onion
Salt and pepper to taste
Parsley, chopped
Butter
½ pint cream
Paprika
Sliced, blanched almonds

Lay filets in a single layer in a flat, well-buttered pyrex dish. Squeeze lemon juice over them. Sprinkle with chopped mushrooms, minced onion, salt, pepper and parsley. Dot with butter and pour cream over all. Bake at 350 degrees for 15 minutes. When done, sprinkle top with paprika and almonds. Put under broiler to brown slightly.

Poultry & Game

Fresh poultry and game were in abundance and hung in the kitchen larder.

BAJA CALIFORNIA CHICKEN

Serves 8

8 boned chicken breasts
Seasoning salt and pepper to taste
2 cloves garlic, crushed
4 tablespoons olive oil
4 tablespoons tarragon vinegar
⅔ cup dry sherry

Sprinkle chicken with seasoning salt and pepper. Crush garlic into oil and vinegar in a skillet. Sauté chicken pieces until golden brown, turning frequently. Remove; place in a baking dish. Pour sherry over pieces and place in a 350 degree over for 10 minutes.

BRUNSWICK STEW

Serves 8 to 10

3½ pound chicken
3 to 4 medium-large onions, chopped
1 #2½ can chopped tomatoes
2 #2 cans drained white shoe-peg corn
1 small piece cooking pork
5 to 6 large white potatoes
Salt to taste
Black pepper to taste
Red pepper to taste
Worcestershire sauce to taste
1 (10 ounce) package frozen tiny white butter beans

Stew chicken in a 5-quart stew pot until done. Remove meat from bones; discard bones and return to chicken broth. Add onions, tomatoes, butter beans, pork and seasonings. Cook for 2 to 3 hours on medium to low heat, then add corn. Add water to pot as needed. Peel, slice and cook potatoes in salted water until done. Then mash and add to mixture. Remove cover from stew to cook down and thicken, stirring frequently. Cook about 1 hour longer. *Fresh vegetables can be used in summer and stew freezes well.*

SOUTHERN POLITICAL RALLY BURGOO

Serves 16 to 18

3 tablespoons oil, divided
1 pound beef shank
1 pound pork shoulder
1 (3 pound) chicken, cut up
3 quarts water
1½ tablespoons salt
3 cups onions, chopped
1 clove garlic, chopped
2 cups potatoes, diced
8 ribs celery, diced
1 (28 ounce) can tomatoes
1 pound carrots, diced
1 (10 ounce) package frozen butter beans
2 green peppers, diced
¼ teaspoon crushed red pepper
¼ teaspoon freshly-ground black pepper
1 small onion
4 cloves
1 bay leaf
2 tablespoons brown sugar
1 (10 ounce) package frozen okra
2 ears corn (cut kernels)
1 stick butter
½ cup flour
1 tablespoon Worcestershire sauce
½ cup parsley, chopped

Heat 1 tablespoon oil in 8-quart pot. Add beef, pork and chicken. Brown on all sides over low heat. Add water and salt. Cook over low heat until just tender, skimming as necessary. Cool. Remove bones and skin; discard. Cut meat into small pieces and return to broth. Heat remaining oil. Cook chopped onion until limp. Add to broth along with garlic, potatoes, celery, tomatoes, carrots, beans, peppers, red and black pepper, onion stuck with 4 cloves, bay leaf and sugar. Cook slowly about 1½ hours, skimming and stirring occasionally. Add okra and corn; cook 15 minutes longer. Knead butter and flour together until well blended. Stir into stew. Cook, stirring, until stew has thickened. Adjust seasonings. Add Worcestershire sauce. Sprinkle with parsley.

...Ham, cold corn beef, cold fowl, red herrings, cold mutton, the dishes ornamented with sprigs of parsley, and other vegetables from the garden.

Manasseh Cutler's Diary, January 2, 1802

CARROLL'S CHICKEN SPAGHETTI

Serves 12 generously

Step I

1 large hen
3 cups water
1 carrot, sliced
1 large onion
1 small green pepper (optional)
2 cloves garlic, chopped
3 ribs celery, with leaves
1 teaspoon salt
4 peppercorns

Cut chicken in pieces. Boil slowly for 2 hours with water, vegetables and seasoning. Remove the chicken and strain the stock. Set aside and let cool. Skim off fat that forms on the top.

Step II

2 small green peppers, cut in small pieces
2 cloves garlic
1 pound fresh mushrooms, cut in pieces
1 (#3) can tomatoes
1 (6 ounce) can tomato paste
2 tablespoons chili powder
⅛ teaspoon cayenne pepper
¼ teaspoon black pepper

Sauté green pepper and garlic in fat removed from chicken stock until lightly brown. Remove garlic. Add all the other ingredients and simmer until well blended.

Step III

Cook 2 to 3 pounds of spaghetti in stock which the chicken has been cooked in, plus enough water to make 3 quarts. Do not overcook. Drain. Cut chicken in bite-size pieces, add to the sauce and mix with the cooked spaghetti.

Step IV

1 pound American cheese
Parmesan cheese

Shred or chop American cheese and add to spaghetti and chicken. Simmer until all cheese is melted. Serve with freshly-grated Parmesan cheese sprinkled on top. *This receipt is better if made in advance and can be kept warm in a double boiler.*

Red Devons in the Paddock

Both gardens and livestock benefited from George Washington's interest in efficiency and scientific agriculture. Unlike many of his contemporaries, he penned his livestock, both as an aid to fattening them for food and to make it easier to collect fertilizer for his fields. These Red Devons, descendants of an 18th century breed, are confined in one of the paddocks at Mount Vernon.

(Photograph by Paul Kennedy)

MARJORAM CHICKEN

Serves 8

1 lemon, halved
Two 3 pound broilers
8 tablespoons butter
2 cloves garlic, minced
8 large mushrooms, sliced
½ teaspoon salt
2 teaspoons marjoram
Pinch nutmeg
Brandy (optional)

Split 2 broilers into quarters or into 8 pieces if you prefer. Rub them with the cut lemon. Melt 6 tablespoons of butter; add the garlic. Broil the chicken on a rack in a roasting pan, basting frequently with the garlic mixture, for 12 to 15 minutes. Meanwhile, sauté the mushrooms for 5 minutes in 2 tablespoons of butter with salt, marjoram and nutmeg. When chicken is golden, remove rack and put chicken down on bottom of pan. Baste again and pour the mushroom mixture over. Bake at 300 degrees for 20 minutes. Arrange on a warm platter on a bed of white rice. Garnish with wedges of red tomatoes and green parsley. If desired, ignite 2 to 3 tablespoons of heated brandy and flame chicken before serving.

CHICKEN A LA VAL

Serves 12

12 large single chicken breasts (with or without bone)
Butter and oil
2 (8 ounce) jars currant jelly
1 cup water
2 tablespoons cornstarch
2 teaspoons allspice
3 tablespoons Worcestershire sauce
4 tablespoons lemon juice
Salt and pepper to taste

Preheat oven to 350 degrees. Heat 3 tablespoons each of butter and oil in a large skillet. Brown each breast on each side and transfer the browned breasts to a large roasting pan. Add more butter and oil if necessary. Season with salt and pepper. Bring remaining ingredients to a boil and pour over the chicken. Cover the pan and bake 25 minutes, basting frequently. Remove the cover and bake 10 minutes longer, basting twice. Serve on a heated platter. Strain a little of the sauce over the chicken and the rest into a sauce bowl. *This sauce is also excellent with ham.*

CHICKEN (OR VEAL) CHASSEUR

Serves 4

1 pound boneless chicken thighs or 1 pound veal off shank or neck
½ ounce butter
2 tablespoons vegetable oil
1 onion, chopped
1 (4 ounce) can mushrooms
½ tablespoon flour
1 cup stock
¾ cup dry white wine
1 small can tomato paste
Bouquet garni

Cut meat into walnut-sized pieces. Sauté in oil and butter until lightly browned. Remove to saucepan. Sauté chopped onions and mushrooms in remaining oil and butter. Sprinkle with flour. Add stock, wine, tomato paste and bouquet garni and pour over meat in saucepan. Cover and simmer 1 to 1½ hours. Serve with rice.

CHICKEN GLORIA

Serves 4 to 6

4 boneless chicken breasts, split
Salt
Pepper
½ stick butter, melted
1 orange
1 lemon
1 cup sour cream
½ pound mushrooms
½ cup dry white wine or sherry
Parsley

Season the chicken breasts with salt and pepper. Brown in a skillet. Put the chicken in an oven-proof dish and add melted butter, orange peel, lemon peel, and some of the juice from both fruits. Bake for 30 minutes at 350 degrees. Remove from oven and add the sour cream, mushrooms and wine. Then bake an additional 10 minutes. When ready, sprinkle with chopped parsley and serve.

LEMON CHICKEN

Serves 6

3 chicken breasts, split, skinned and boned

Marinade

¼ teaspoon salt
¼ teaspoon pepper
2 tablespoons dry sherry or white wine
½ cup fresh lemon juice (reserve rind for grating)

Combine all the above ingredients to make marinade. Soak chicken breasts in marinade for approximately 2 hours.

Coating

1 egg white
½ cup all-purpose flour
½ cup cornstarch
½ cup water
1½ cups cooking oil

Mix egg white, flour, cornstarch and water. Coat chicken pieces with flour mixture and fry in medium-hot oil until lightly browned. Drain and cut into small pieces.

Sauce

2 tablespoons vegetable oil
4 tablespoons tomato catsup
4 tablespoons soy sauce
1 tablespoon sesame oil
3 tablespoons sugar
½ teaspoon chopped garlic
½ teaspoon chopped ginger
2 to 3 drops hot chili oil
Grated rind 1 lemon
2 tablespoons roasted sesame seeds

Mix together oil, catsup, soy sauce, sesame oil, sugar, chopped ginger, hot chili oil and grated lemon rind. Pour over chicken pieces and place on serving platter. Surround with shredded lettuce, chopped scallions and sprinkle with roasted sesame seeds. Good hot or cold.

HERBED CHICKEN BREASTS PARMESAN

Serves 12

1½ cups fresh bread crumbs
¾ cup grated Parmesan cheese
¼ cup chopped parsley
Pinch garlic powder
1 teaspoon oregano
½ teaspoon basil
Fresh ground pepper
1 teaspoon salt
6 whole, boned chicken breasts cut in half (12 pieces)
¼ pound butter or margarine, melted

Mix all dry ingredients together. Dip breasts in margarine, then in crumb mixture. Arrange on large flat rimmed baking tin. Bake at 350 degrees for 1 hour. Baste with juices from pan.

SAUTÉED TARRAGON CHICKEN

Serves 6-8

8 boneless chicken breast halves
4 tablespoons butter
1 tablespoon oil
Salt and pepper to taste
1 tablespoon dried tarragon
1 tablespoon minced shallots or green onions
½ cup beef stock or bouillon
1 cup whipping cream

Dry chicken pieces thoroughly with paper towels. Heat 2 tablespoons of the butter plus the oil in a sauté pan. Sauté the chicken pieces over moderately high heat until they are golden brown all over. Salt and pepper the chicken, sprinkle with ½ tablespoon of the tarragon, cover pan and continue to cook for 20 minutes, turning and basting the pieces frequently. When the chicken tests done (the juices will run yellow, not pink, when pricked with a fork), place it on a platter and keep warm. Pour out all but 1 tablespoon of the cooking fat. Add shallots and cook over moderate heat, stirring constantly, for 1 minute. Add bouillon and boil down to about 4 tablespoons, scraping up the pan juices. Add cream and allow to boil just enough to coat the spoon lightly. Remove from heat and swirl in remaining butter. Stir in the remaining tarragon. Return the chicken to the sauté pan and baste with the sauce.

TOUCH OF MUSTARD BROILED CHICKEN

Serves 4

3 tablespoons Dijon mustard
½ cup chopped onions
3 tablespoons soy sauce
2 tablespoons margarine
2 tablespoons brown sugar
1 frying chicken, quartered
½ teaspoon salt
½ teaspoon pepper

Preheat the broiler. Combine mustard, onions and soy sauce and spin in blender. In small pan melt margarine, stir in brown sugar. Add the mustard mixture and stir well. Brush sauce on chicken, sprinkle on salt and pepper. Place on a rack in a broiling pan. Broil 20 to 25 minutes with flame set low, turning and basting occasionally, until tender and browned to desired state. Deglaze broiling pan with chicken broth and serve as a gravy.

CHICKEN VERMOUTH

Serves 4

1 (9 ounce) package frozen artichoke hearts
2 tablespoons water
1 teaspoon salt
¼ teaspoon pepper
4 boned single chicken breasts
½ teaspoon oregano
4 strips bacon
½ cup dry vermouth

Separate frozen artichoke hearts. Place in single layer in shallow baking dish. Add the water, salt and pepper. Place chicken breasts, skin side up, completely covering artichoke hearts. Sprinkle with more salt and pepper and the oregano. Top with bacon strips. Add the vermouth, pouring a little over the top of each chicken breast. Bake at 350 degrees about 1 hour or until tender. Add more vermouth for basting if necessary.

POULTRY HASH

Serves 4

2 cups leftover chicken or turkey, cut up
1 small onion, chopped
2 tablespoons butter
2 tablespoons flour
1 cup chicken broth
Salt and pepper

Sauté onions until clear in butter. Add meat, sprinkle with flour, stir and brown. Add broth and stir until thickened to consistency of cream sauce. Season to taste. Delicious with batter bread or waffles. *Beef can be used in place of chicken or turkey.*

GOLDEN TURKEY PIE

Serves 4 to 6

1 deep-dish 9-inch pie shell
1 cup chopped celery
1 tablespoon butter or margarine
1 cup diced, cooked turkey
2 tablespoons chopped pimento
3 eggs
1 cup milk
¼ cup mayonnaise
2 tablespoons prepared yellow mustard
½ teaspoon salt
1 cup shredded Cheddar or Monterey Jack cheese
Paprika

Preheat empty cookie sheet in 375 degree oven. Add pie shell to hot cookie sheet and bake for 10 minutes. (This will make it crisp.) Cook celery in butter until tender; stir in turkey and pimento. Beat together eggs, milk, mayonnaise, mustard and salt. Stir in turkey mixture. Pour into pie shell. Sprinkle with cheese and paprika. Bake at 375 degrees for 25 to 35 minutes, until silver knife inserted near center comes out clean.

COLD SLICED TURKEY TONNATO

Serves 6

5 to 6 tablespoons flour
½ teaspoon salt
Several grinds whole pepper
12 slices fresh turkey breast
4 tablespoons butter

Mix flour, salt and pepper. Lightly dust turkey slices with seasoned flour. Melt butter in frying pan. Cook turkey slices 2 to 3 minutes on each side. Remove to platter, slightly overlapping, and let cool.

Sauce

1 (7 ounce) can tuna fish with oil
1 (2 ounce) can anchovy filets with oil
2 cups dry white wine
2 to 3 cups strong chicken stock
¼ teaspoon sage
¼ teaspoon thyme
¼ teaspoon white pepper
1½ cups mayonnaise
Juice 1 lemon
2 tablespoons capers

Purée in blender the tuna fish, anchovies, wine, lemon juice and all seasonings. Combine the purée and mayonnaise. Add enough chicken stock to make a smooth sauce as thick as mayonnaise. Stir in capers. Taste and adjust seasoning. Pour sauce over turkey slices. Garnish as desired and serve cold.

CORNISH HENS MARENGO

Serves 4

4 fresh cornish game hens
Salt and pepper
2 tablespoons butter
1 cup chopped fresh tomatoes
1 cup sliced fresh mushrooms
1 medium onion, chopped
1 clove garlic, minced
1 teaspoon Italian seasoning
½ cup dry white wine
¼ cup grated Parmesan cheese
¼ cup sliced stuffed olives

Pat hens dry and season inside and out with salt and pepper. Fold wings back and tie legs together. Brown hens in butter in skillet. Add tomatoes, mushrooms, onion, garlic, seasoning and wine. Bring to a boil. Cover, reduce heat and simmer 45 minutes or until hens are tender. Remove to serving platter. Add cheese and olives to the sauce. Heat and spoon over and around the hens.

GRILLED BREASTS OF DOVE

Serves 6 to 8 as main course
Serves 12 as appetizer

24 dove breasts
12 slices bacon

Marinade I
1 bottle Italian salad dressing or

Marinade II
9 tablespoons red wine
¾ cup oil
⅔ cup garlic vinegar
1 teaspoon dry mustard
6 tablespoons soy sauce
¼ cup Worcestershire sauce
¼ teaspoon salt
½ teaspoon pepper
1 teaspoon Italian seasonings

Clean dove breasts, being careful to remove any hidden buckshot. Halve strips of bacon. Wrap each breast with bacon. Secure strip by inserting toothpick laterally through the strip and breast. Prepare marinade by combining all ingredients. Mix well. Pour over doves and cover. Refrigerate for at least 6 hours. To grill, cook slowly over charcoal fire, turning frequently. Cook approximately 30 minutes. Fire should be about 6 to 8 inches away from birds. To smoke, place dove on upper grill. Pour marinade into water pan containing appropriate amounts of water for smoker. Cook for 1 to 1½ hours.

POTTED DOVES

Serves 3

6 doves
1 small onion, sliced
3 tablespoons Worcestershire sauce
Red pepper or hot sauce (small amount)
Salt and pepper
1 cup catsup
1 tablespoon butter
6 slices bacon

Steam birds for 20 minutes on top of stove with a little water. Then add seasoning and catsup. Dot with butter and lay bacon on top of the birds. Cook covered for about 1½ hours or until very tender. Remove cover and brown in oven.

TEXAS DOVES

Serves 6

12 doves
1 teaspoon salt
1 tablespoon heavy cracked pepper
¼ pound butter
2¾ cups chicken broth, homemade or canned
1½ tablespoons arrowroot flour
½ cup dry white wine, optional

Sprinkle each dove with salt and coarse pepper. Melt butter in a 10-inch heavy frying pan. Place seasoned doves in frying pan and brown on all sides. After the doves are well browned, pour over 2 cups of the chicken broth. Cover tightly and simmer over low heat for 1½ hours. Remove the birds to a heated platter. Mix the flour into ¾ cup of the chicken broth and stir until blended. Add to the contents of the frying pan and stir with a fork, scraping all the juices adhering to the pan. If desired, add ½ cup dry white wine to give extra flavor. Stir until slightly thickened. Pour through a strainer over the birds. *Birds may be tenderized, if desired, by soaking them in milk for 2 hours before cooking.*

ROASTED WILD DUCK

Clean, wipe and dry the ducks. Sprinkle generously with flour, salt and pepper. Place whole peeled onion inside each duck and place them in self-basting roaster. Fasten with toothpicks 2 or 3 strips of bacon across each bird. If desired, ducks may be stuffed with wild rice dressing made by boiling wild rice and seasoning with salt, pepper and chopped onion. Cover bottom of roaster with water. Cover tightly and roast in oven at 350 degrees for 2 hours. Remove cover of roaster for last 20 minutes before taking from oven to allow skin to brown.

ROAST WILD GOOSE

Serves 4 to 6

4 to 6 pound goose
Salt
Pepper
1 or 2 raw white potatoes, peeled
¼ pound soft butter or margarine
⅔ cup water
⅓ cup dry gin

Wash inside of goose with running water. Dry and shake in salt and pepper. Stuff with raw potatoes, cut to size if necessary. If skin of goose is torn or missing, cover with strips of bacon held in place with toothpicks. Rub outside of goose with butter or margarine. Place on rack in roasting pan to which water and gin have been added. Cover and roast at 350 degrees for about 2 hours, a little less for a smaller bird, a little more for a larger one. Baste every 15 minutes or so with pan drippings, adding more gin and water as necessary. Serve with Savory Orange Sauce.

Savory Orange Sauce

1 cup fresh squeezed orange juice
¾ cup dark brown sugar
1 teaspoon white sugar
1 heaping teaspoon cornstarch
1 tablespoon grated orange peel
2 to 3 drops TABASCO brand pepper sauce
1 ounce cointreau

Combine all ingredients except cointreau and cook over low heat until sauce is thick and clear. Remove from heat and stir in cointreau. Makes about 1 cup of sauce. *This sauce is also excellent with other wild game meats.*

ROASTED PHEASANTS OR CORNISH HENS

Serves 8

4 young pheasants or cornish hens
2 pounds white seedless grapes
1 can mushroom soup
2 cans cut mushrooms or 1 pound fresh mushrooms
2 ounces sherry

Preheat oven to 500 degrees. Stuff the prepared birds with grapes or lacking those with white raisins that have been plumped in white wine or water. Place the birds in a roasting pan and put in a preheated oven to brown. When the birds are brown, turn the heat down to 325 degrees. Cover with soup, mushrooms and wine. Cover and cook 2½ hours or until tender. Pheasants will take longer than the chicken.

ROAST QUAIL

1 bird serves 1 person

Clean quail. Wrap them in grape leaves and then in slices of bacon. Tie with string. Place in roasting pan. Spread with a little butter and put in a very hot oven (450 degrees). Cook 15 minutes, basting frequently. Remove from pan. Make gravy by adding a little water to the pan. Cook and stir in all the browned juice in the bottom of the pan. If desired, add 1 tablespoon dry sherry and ¼ cup white seedless grapes to gravy *for each quail cooked.* Serve each bird on a round of toast spread with liver patė. Accompany with wild rice.

SOUTHERN FRIED QUAIL

Dry pick quail. Clean and wipe thoroughly. Sprinkle with salt and pepper and dredge with flour. Have a heavy deep-frying pan with tight-fitting lid half full of hot fat. Put in quail, cook for a few minutes over a hot fire, then cover skillet and reduce heat. Cook slowly until tender, turning the quail to the other side when golden brown. Serve on hot platter with slices of lemon and sprigs of parsley.

VENISON BOURGIGNON

Serves 6

2 pounds lean venison (fat completely removed), cut into ½ inch cubes
2 tablespoons butter
2 tablespoons sherry, heated
24 small white onions or 1 (16 ounce) package frozen onions, thawed and drained
12 large mushrooms, quartered
1 teaspoon tomato paste
1 teaspoon meat glaze (Bovril or other concentrate)
3 tablespoons flour
½ cup beef consommé or more to taste
½ cup red wine or more to taste
Salt and pepper
Bouquet garni (1 small bay leaf, 2 sprigs each thyme and marjoram tied in cheesecloth or bottled bouquet garni to taste)
2 tablespoons parsley, chopped

Brown meat quickly in hot fat in a heavy skillet or casserole and pour sherry over it. Transfer to medium casserole with a slotted spoon. Salt lightly. In fat remaining in skillet sauté onions and mushrooms lightly. Stir in tomato paste, meat glaze and flour. Add consommé and red wine slowly, stirring until it comes to a boil. Season to taste and pour over venison in casserole. Add bouquet garni, cover and cook in very slow oven (250 degrees) about 3 hours or until meat is very tender. Add more wine and/or consommé at intervals while casserole is cooking, according to need or personal taste. Sprinkle with parsley before serving.

Washington's marble mortar.

VENISON WITH SOUR CREAM

Serves 4 to 6

2 pounds venison
½ cup fat
1 clove garlic
1 cup diced celery
½ cup minced onion
1 bay leaf
4 tablespoons butter
1 cup diced carrots
2 cups water
1 teaspoon salt
4 tablespoons flour
1 cup sour cream

Cut venison in pieces. Melt fat in heavy frying pan. Add meat and garlic. Brown on all sides and arrange in oven-serving dish. Put vegetables in remaining fat and cook for 2 minutes. Add salt, pepper and water. Pour over meat. Bake in slow oven (250 degrees) until meat is tender (2 to 3 hours). Drain and reserve the liquid. Melt butter in frying pan and stir in flour. Add water that the meat was cooked in and boil until thick. Add sour cream and more salt if necessary. Pour over meat and vegetables. Serve with buttered noodles and currant jelly.

FRUIT DRESSING FOR YOUR HOLIDAY BIRD

Serves 14 to 16

2 cups chopped, unpeeled Jonathan apples
2 cups chopped celery
2 cups chopped, seeded dates
2 cups chopped figs
2 cups mixed nuts (Brazil, walnuts, filberts and pecans)
1 cup grape juice
6 slices buttered toasted bread, cut into cubes
1 cup turkey drippings

Mix apples, celery, dates, figs, nutmeats and toasted bread cubes. Moisten with grape juice. Arrange ingredients in a 9x13-inch pyrex dish. Baste with turkey drippings. Bake at 350 degrees for 30 to 45 minutes.

Meats, Stews

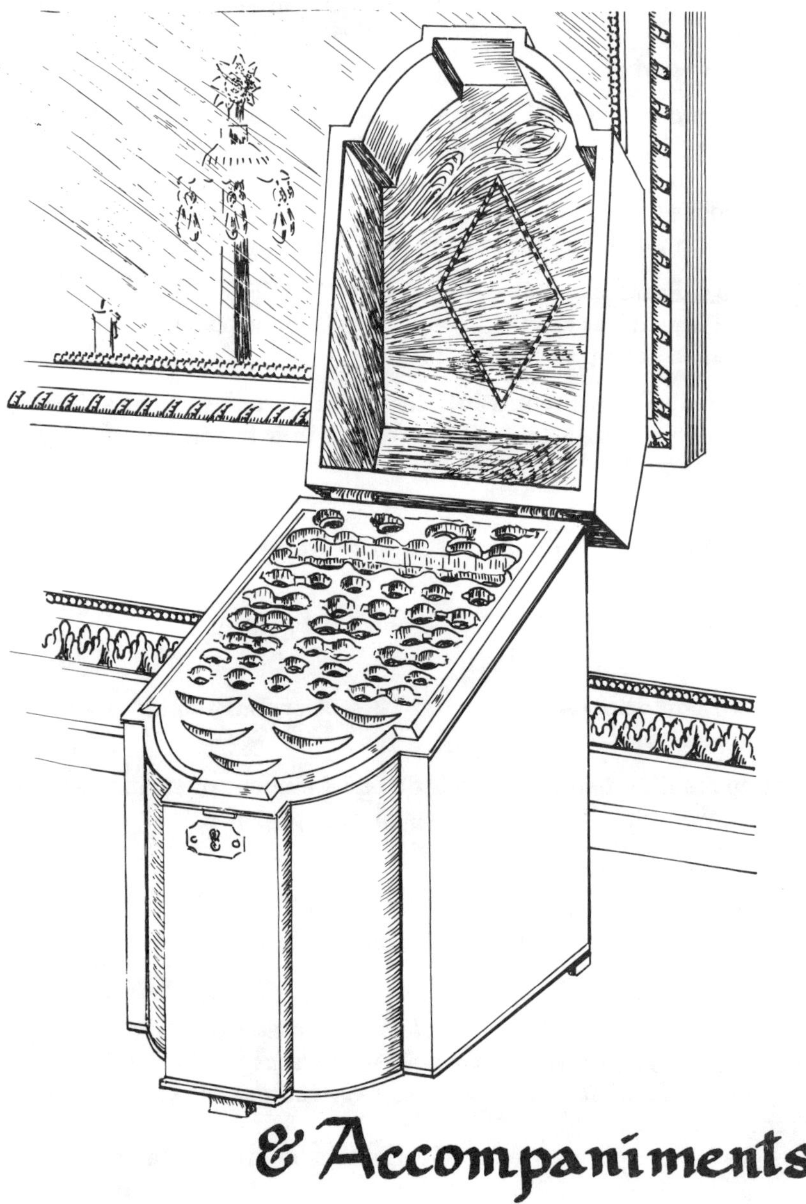

& Accompaniments

An original knifebox on the sideboard in the Large Dining Room. Three or four meats were served at dinner and each guest chose his favorite.

FILET DE BOEUF MARIE-LOUISE

Filet of beef
Salt
Pepper
Artichoke hearts
Fresh mushroom purée
Onion purée
Glazed carrots

After having larded a filet of beef (tenderloin), season with salt and pepper and tie with a string to help it keep its correct shape during cooking. Roast in a hot oven (450 degrees). Allow 12 to 15 minutes per pound. When cooked, garnish with artichoke hearts filled with mushroom purée, onion purée and glazed carrots.

Mushroom Purée

½ pound mushrooms, finely chopped in food processor
2 to 3 tablespoons butter

Wring chopped mushrooms in a tea towel to remove excess moisture. Sauté them in 2 to 3 tablespoons butter in a frying pan until pieces separate, about 5 to 6 minutes.

Onion Purée

1 pound onions, puréed in food processor
3 to 4 tablespoons butter

Sauté onions in butter in a frying pan until golden.

Gravy

Deglazed pan drippings
Strong beef stock
2 tablespoons tomato paste

Deglaze roasting pan; measure. Add equal amount of strong beef stock and mix well. Stir in 2 tablespoons of tomato paste.

...Having good meats for my Table by the middle of March, and in succession through the year, according to the seasons, is highly proper & very desirable, as it has always been my custom to supply it with the best...

George Washington to James Anderson
January 15, 1797

BEEF FILET IN A CRUST

Serves 4

Pastry crust sufficient for one 2-crust 9-inch pie
1½ pounds beef tenderloin
Salt
Pepper
2 cloves garlic, pressed
½ pound mushrooms
Butter (approximately ⅓ pound)
½ cup (or more) sherry

Divide the pastry into 2 parts and roll each about ¼ inch thick. Place on cookie sheet. Season the steak with salt, pepper and pressed garlic. Clean and slice the mushrooms. Sauté the meat in some of the butter over a very high flame on both sides. Remove from the pan. Add more butter and sauté the mushrooms. Remove them from the pan. Add more butter and the wine. Reduce it by half by cooking rapidly. Place the meat on 1 pastry round. Top with the mushrooms and the sauce. Cover with the other round. Fold and seal the edges tightly. Bake at 375 degrees for 25 to 30 minutes. Serve plain or with a Béarnaise sauce.

FILETS MIGNON, SHALLOT SAUCE

Serves 4

4 tablespoons butter
4 filets of beef, 1 inch thick
Salt
Pepper
2 tablespoons shallots, chopped
½ cup dry white wine
Parsley

Melt 3 tablespoons butter in a skillet; brown meat for 4 minutes on each side over high heat. Season with salt and pepper. Place on hot platter and keep warm. To the pan juices in skillet add shallots, wine and remaining tablespoon of butter. Mix well and cook over medium heat for 2 minutes. Spoon over filets. Garnish with chopped parsley.
Onions may be substituted for shallots.

BRANDIED SIRLOIN STEAK

Serves 3 to 4

4 tablespoons butter
TABASCO brand pepper sauce
Juice 1 lemon
1½ pounds sirloin steak
Worcestershire sauce
1 teaspoon oregano
½ cup brandy

Melt the butter in a heavy skillet. Add about ½ teaspoon of Tabasco sauce and the lemon juice. Brown the steak on both sides over high heat. Cover and continue cooking until done to your liking. Just before serving, pour on a couple of tablespoons of Worcestershire; sprinkle with the oregano and the brandy.

BEEF BRISKET

Serves 6 to 8

3 pound brisket, fat removed
1 package onion soup mix
½ cup red wine
2 tablespoons flour
⅓ cup prepared horseradish (optional)

Place brisket in large piece of heavy foil in large pan. Sprinkle onion soup mix on top and pour over the red wine. Wrap up foil tightly. Put in 325 degree oven and cook 3½ hours. When done, pour off liquid, strain (add the horseradish if you wish) and thicken with the flour. Taste for seasoning. Pass sauce with sliced meat.

HANOVER'S EASY BRISKET

Serves 8 to 10

1 can consommé
1 small bottle soy sauce
1 tablespoon liquid smoke
1 or 2 cloves garlic, pressed
4 or 5 pound brisket
½ cup bottled barbeque sauce

Combine all ingredients except barbecue sauce, pour over meat and marinate overnight. Cover with foil and bake in liquid for 4 hours for 4 pounds or 5 hours for 5 pounds at 300 degrees. Baste occasionally during baking, adding more consommé if necessary. Cover until last hour of total time and then remove cover and pour ½ cup bottled barbecue sauce over brisket and increase oven temperature to 350 degrees.

EFFORTLESS OVEN BEEF STEW

Serves 6 to 8

2 pounds stewing beef
1 onion
3 stalks celery
6 carrots, sliced
2 tablespoons tapioca
1 tablespoon sugar
2 teaspoons salt
Few peppercorns
½ bay leaf
4 ounces tomato juice

Cube beef. Slice onion thin. Cut celery diagonally into small pieces. Combine all ingredients. Bake 4 hours in 250 degree oven in covered casserole. No browning of meat is necessary. Meat browns as it cooks and sauce thickens itself.

GREEK BEEF STEW

Serves 8

3 pounds lean beef, cubed
Salt
Pepper
½ cup butter
2½ pounds small white onions, peeled
¼ pound mushrooms, chopped
1 (6 ounce) can tomato paste
⅓ cup red wine
2 tablespoons red wine vinegar
1 tablespoon brown sugar
1 clove garlic, mashed
1 bay leaf
1 small stick cinnamon
½ teaspoon whole cloves
¼ teaspoon cumin
2 tablespoons currants or raisins

Season meat well with salt and pepper. Melt butter in heavy kettle with cover. Add meat and coat with butter but do not brown. Arrange onions and mushrooms over meat. Mix together tomato paste, wine, vinegar, brown sugar and garlic. Pour over meat. Add bay leaf, cinnamon, cloves, cumin and currants. Cover and simmer 3 hours. Do not stir until serving time. Serve with noodles sprinkled with sesame seeds.

LOUISIANA COUNTRY STEW

Serves 6 to 8

3 pounds beef stew meat
½ teaspoon celery salt
¼ teaspoon garlic salt
½ teaspoon ginger
1 (16 ounce) can tomatoes
3 medium or 6 small onions
⅓ cup red wine vinegar
½ cup molasses
3 or 4 cups chunked carrots
½ cup raisins
Kneaded butter (3 tablespoons flour mixed with 2 tablespoons butter)

Brown the cubed meat in Dutch oven. Add celery salt, garlic salt, pepper and ginger. Add tomatoes, onions, red wine vinegar and molasses. Simmer, covered, for 2 hours. The last ½ hour add cut up carrots and raisins. Thicken with kneaded butter dropped by bits into the sauce and whisked until smooth. Serve over rice. Accompany with a large batch of corn bread.

MEAT BALLS IN CURRY SAUCE

Serves 6 to 8

1½ pounds ground beef
¾ cup rolled oats
1 cup milk
1 egg
⅓ cup finely chopped onion
2 teaspoons salt
⅛ teaspoon pepper
¼ cup butter or margarine

Combine first 7 ingredients. Mix well. Melt butter in large frying pan. Spoon rounded tablespoons of meat mixture into frying pan. Cook and brown on all sides, turning as needed. Remove from pan, place in casserole and keep warm. Make sauce.

Sauce

2 tablespoons butter
⅓ cup chopped onion
⅓ cup chopped celery
3 tablespoons flour
1 tablespoon curry powder
1 teaspoon salt
2 cups milk
2 whole cloves
1 package frozen peas, partially defrosted
1 tablespoon lemon juice

Cook celery and onions in butter until tender, not brown. Blend in flour, curry powder and salt. Add milk. Stir constantly until thick and smooth. Add peas and lemon juice to browned meat balls. Add sauce. Bake at 350 degrees for 10 to 15 minutes.

SUNFLOWER STUFFED PEPPERS

Serves 4

4 medium green peppers, halved and seeded
½ pound ground beef
1 egg
2 cups cooked brown rice
1 teaspoon prepared horseradish
1 teaspoon tamari
1 cup shredded Swiss or Cheddar cheese
1 cup tomato sauce (8 ounce can)
3 tablespoons sunflower seeds

Steam the peppers for 5 minutes. Arrange them, cut side up, in a shallow baking dish. Sauté ground beef in a skillet until cooked through. In a large bowl beat the egg slightly and add the rice, ground beef, horseradish, tamari and half of the cheese. Mix together lightly and pile into pepper shells. Bake at 350 degrees for 15 minutes. Remove from oven, pour tomato sauce over the tops, sprinkle with remaining ½ cup cheese and the sunflower seeds and return to the oven for 15 minutes more.

HAM CALVADOS

Serves 8

2 oranges
1 lemon
1 teaspoon ginger
½ teaspoon nutmeg
1 cup dark brown sugar
1 (16 ounce) can pitted black cherries
½ cup Madeira
6 pound fresh ham
½ cup Calvados
Fresh parsley

Preheat the oven to 325 degrees. Grate the rinds of the oranges and lemon and squeeze the juice. In a small saucepan combine the gratings, juice, ginger, nutmeg, brown sugar, the juice drained from the cherries and the Madeira. Simmer for 3 to 4 minutes, stirring frequently. Wipe the ham and score it into diamonds. Place on a rack in an open roasting pan. Pour over the syrup. Bake for 40 minutes per pound, basting every 20 minutes with the pan drippings. Fifteen minutes before the end of cooking, pour over the Calvados and baste every 5 minutes with the drippings. Transfer the ham to a platter and let stand 20 minutes. Spoon off the excess fat from the sauce and pour the pan juices into a small saucepan. Add the cherries and simmer 5 minutes. To serve, pour some of the sauce and cherries over the ham and surround it with a ring of parsley sprigs. Serve the rest of the sauce in a separate bowl.

FRESH HAM MARSALA

Serves 8

12 pound fresh ham
Vinegar
2 cloves garlic, crushed
1 bottle Marsala wine
1 cup water
Brown sugar

Rub ham with vinegar and garlic cloves. Place in a casserole and pour 1 bottle of Marsala over it. Add water and sprinkle with brown sugar. Wrap ham in foil and cook in a slow oven (325 degrees) 25 minutes per pound.

MUSTARD SAUCE FOR HAM

Yield: 1½ cups

½ cup brown sugar
½ cup vinegar
¼ cup dry mustard
½ cup butter
3 egg yolks

Put all ingredients in double boiler and cook, stirring constantly, until mixture is consistency of custard. Chill and serve with ham. Can be reheated in double boiler, stirring to prevent curdling.

INDIVIDUAL HAM LOAVES

Serves 8

1 pound smoked ham, ground
¾ pound fresh pork, ground
¾ pound veal, ground
2 cups bread crumbs
1 cup milk
2 eggs, beaten
Salt and pepper to taste

Mix well and form into 8 individual loaves. Place in shallow baking pan and pour over the following sauce which has been mixed and heated.

Sauce
1½ cups brown sugar
½ cup water
½ cup white vinegar
1 teaspoon dry mustard
½ cup medium dry sherry

Bake in 300 degree to 325 degree oven for 1½ hours, basting several times. Add more water and sherry if necessary. Do not allow sauce to thicken and burn.

SUPERLATIVE HAM LOAF

Serves 12

3 pounds smoked lean ham
1½ pounds lean pork
1 pound ground beef
1 cup dried fine bread crumbs
2 eggs
1 (16 ounce) can tomato wedges
¼ cup dark brown sugar
2 teaspoons creamed horseradish
½ teaspoon dry mustard
2 teaspoons salt
2 teaspoons pepper

Have butcher grind ham, pork and beef together. Place meat in very large bowl or roaster. Beat eggs. Add crumbs, tomatoes, salt, pepper, brown sugar, horseradish and mustard. When well mixed add this "stew" to meat mixture. Mix thoroughly, preferably by hand. Form into 1 large loaf or 2 smaller ones (1 for the freezer). Bake uncovered for 2 hours at 350 degrees. Serve with horseradish sauce or mustard sauce. *Delicious hot or cold.*

NEW ENGLAND HAM LOAF AND SWEET-SOUR SAUCE

Serves 6 to 8

1 pound ground ham
1 pound ground pork
1 cup rye or whole wheat bread crumbs
2 eggs
1 cup sour cream
1 tablespoon lemon juice
2 tablespoons minced onion
1 teaspoon curry powder
1 teaspoon powered ginger
1 teaspoon dry mustard
¼ teaspoon ground nutmeg

Combine the ingredients and shape into a loaf or bake in a large loaf pan. Bake at 350 degrees for 1 hour, covering the meat after ½ hour. Serve with the following sweet-sour sauce, which may be poured over the loaf 10 minutes before taking from the oven to better meld the juices. *This pleasantly pungent party loaf is a whiz to make in a food processor but take care not to over process and do the meats separately.*

Sweet-Sour Sauce
1 cup cider vinegar
1 cup water
1 tablespoon lemon juice
1 cup brown sugar
1 tablespoon dry mustard

Simmer the ingredients together for 10 to 15 minutes until the sauce is slightly syrupy.

HAM WITH GREEN NOODLES AND PEAS

Serves 8 to 10

1 pound cooked ham, cut ½ inch thick
¾ pound green peas (may be frozen)
½ pound butter
2 pounds green noodles (homemade if possible)
2 cups heavy cream
½ cup freshly grated Parmesan cheese
Salt
Pepper
Pinch nutmeg

Cut the ham in thin 1-inch strips. Sauté the peas in a heavy skillet in a little butter. Add the ham and heat. Cook the noodles until just done in plenty of salted water. Drain. Have a large casserole ready with the rest of the butter and the cream heated on low heat. Put in the noodles; stir. Add the peas, ham and ½ of the Parmesan. Mix well. Serve with more cheese on the side.

SWEDISH HAM BALLS

Serves 4

2½ cups ground ham
2 cups fresh bread crumbs
2 eggs, well beaten
1 cup milk
1 cup brown sugar
1 teaspoon dry mustard
½ cup white vinegar
½ cup water

Combine meat, bread crumbs, eggs and milk. Form into 12 to 16 large balls and place in a 1½-quart flat casserole. Combine sugar, mustard, vinegar and water. Stir until sugar dissolves. Pour over ham balls. Bake at 325 degrees for 1 hour.

HOWARD HAM SAUCE

Yield: 1½ cups

½ pint heavy cream
½ cup sugar
½ cup white vinegar
2 tablespoons dry mustard
½ teaspoon salt
4 egg yolks, beaten

Put first 5 ingredients in double boiler. Stir. When hot, slowly add the beaten yolks, beating constantly until it thickens. Serve with baked ham or baked ham slice.

VEAL KIDNEYS IN MUSTARD CREAM SAUCE

Serves 4 to 6

2 veal kidneys (1 pound each)
2 cups beef stock or consommé
2 tablespoons minced shallots or green onion
12 ounces mushrooms
4 tablespoons butter
4 tablespoons oil
½ cup Madeira
1 cup heavy cream
1 tablespoon Dijon mustard
Salt
Pepper
Chopped parsley

Remove the membrane and fat from the kidneys. Place in a pan and cover with beef stock, adding water if necessary. Bring to a boil, remove from heat and allow to cool, reserving stock. Cut the kidneys into thin slices. Peel and mince the shallots. Wash the mushrooms briefly and slice them quite thin. Heat the butter and oil in a large skillet. When sizzling hot, add the mushrooms and kidneys and stir for 1 minute. Remove from the heat and reduce the heat to medium-low. Add the shallots and cook over heat for 1 minute. Add 2 cups of the reserved broth, the Madeira and the cream. Simmer 10 minutes. Just before serving, stir in the mustard and season with salt and pepper. Serve in warm patty shells or on toast. Sprinkle with chopped parsley.

KIDNEY STEW FOR SUNDAY BREAKFAST

Serves 6 to 8

8 lamb kidneys
2 eggs, hard-boiled
½ pint cream
4 tablespoons butter
4 tablespoons flour
Salt
Pepper

Cover kidneys with water and simmer 15 minutes. Reserve water. Make a cream sauce by melting butter, stirring in flour and adding cream plus 1 cup of water in which kidneys were boiled, strained. Wash kidneys and slice into cream sauce. Add salt and pepper to taste. A small chopped onion may be added for Sunday night supper.

ROLLED LEG OF LAMB

Serves 8

6 pound leg of lamb
⅓ cup prepared mustard
2 tablespoons soy sauce
1 tablespoon rosemary
2 tablespoons safflower oil
¼ teaspoon ginger

Order the leg boned and rolled. Keep the bones. Mix the remaining ingredients and brush all over the lamb, preferably the morning before serving to allow the flavors to penetrate. Roast the lamb at 325 degrees for 1½ to 1¾ hours, depending on desired pinkness. Put the bones in the roasting pan for added flavor.

LEG OF LAMB WITH SPICY SAUCE

Serves 8

7 pound leg of lamb
Salt
Pepper
1 bottle chili sauce
6 tablespoons Worcestershire sauce
4 tablespoons vinegar
4 large onions, finely chopped
3 or 4 green peppers, finely chopped
1 clove garlic, mashed (optional)
1 tablespoon thyme
3 cans beef stock

Mix together the chili sauce, Worcestershire, vinegar, onion, green pepper, garlic, thyme and beef stock. Season the lamb with salt and pepper and place in a roasting pan. Pour the combined mixture over the lamb and roast at 325 degrees, covered, for 2½ to 3 hours, depending upon the size of the lamb. Baste frequently. Remove lamb from roasting pan. Remove fat from the sauce. If desired, the sauce can be put in a blender and blended until smooth. Serve the sauce with slices of the lamb. *This can be prepared in the morning. Leave the lamb at room temperature, then reheat in the oven before serving.*

LAMB AND VEGETABLE STEW

Serves 6 to 8

3 pounds shoulder of lamb, cubed
2 medium onions, sliced
2 cloves garlic, chopped
3 (8 ounce) cans tomato sauce
½ cup water
½ teaspoon dried rosemary
½ teaspoon dried thyme
¾ teaspoon dried sweet basil
¼ teaspoon pepper
½ pound green beans, cut
1 green pepper, seeded and diced
1 small eggplant, unpeeled and cubed
2 medium zucchini, sliced
¼ cup chopped parsley

Place 3 pounds cubed lamb in a heavy casserole and brown in its own fat. Remove meat and brown sliced onions and garlic in remaining fat for about 2 minutes. Drain off any excess fat. Replace meat; add tomato sauce, water, rosemary, thyme, basil and pepper and simmer, covered, for 1 hour. Add beans and green pepper and simmer another 15 minutes. Add eggplant, zucchini and parsley, stir well and simmer, covered, 30 minutes longer. Serve from casserole with noodles or wild rice.

LAMB AND RICE CASSEROLE

Serves 6

2 cups cooked lamb, cut in cubes
2 cups meat stock
4 tomatoes, peeled and chopped
2 onions, grated
Salt
Pepper
3 tablespoons butter
½ cup raw rice
2 tablespoons Worcestershire sauce

Preheat oven to 325 dgrees. Cook first 4 ingredients over very low flame for 15 minutes. Do not boil. Season lightly with salt and pepper and set aside. In a frying pan, melt the butter and stir in raw rice. Cook until nicely browned. Add Worcestershire sauce. Combine rice and lamb and turn mixture into well-buttered casserole. Bake for 35 to 40 minutes.

ORANGE LAMB STEW

Serves 6 to 8

3 pounds boneless lean lamb shoulder, cut in 1-inch cubes, dredged in flour lightly
3 large carrots, peeled and cut in 1-inch pieces
2 stalks celery, coarsely chopped
2 leeks, well washed and coarsely chopped
2 cloves garlic, minced
1½ cups dry white wine
¼ cup olive oil
1½ cups fresh orange juice
Salt
Pepper
3 parsley sprigs, 3 strips orange peel and 2 bay leaves, wrapped in a small bag of cheesecloth
4 teaspoons sugar
3 large navel oranges
2 tablespoons minced orange peel
2 tablespoons minced parsley
2 teaspoons minced garlic (additional to above)

In large heat-proof casserole cook carrots, celery, leeks and 2 cloves garlic in ¼ cup of olive oil over low heat for 10 minutes or until vegetables are soft and golden. Transfer with slotted spoon to a dish. Add lamb to casserole in batches and sear over high heat, adding more olive oil if necessary and turning frequently, approximately 2 minutes or until it is well browned. Add wine and orange juice and bring the liquid to a boil. Return vegetables to casserole and season the mixture with salt and pepper to taste. Add bag with parsley, bay leaves and rind. *Simmer* the stew, covered, over very low heat for 1 hour. In a small heavy saucepan cook 4 teaspoons of sugar over low heat, stirring until it has caramelized and then add ½ cup of the cooking liquid from the stew in a stream, stirring until smooth. Pour into casserole and continue simmering covered stew 1 hour longer or until meat is tender. Strain cooking liquid into a saucepan, pressing hard on the vegetables. Simmer for 5 minutes and skim off fat. Return liquid and the lamb (throw away vegetables) to casserole. Add 3 large navel oranges, peeled and cut into sections. Bring stew to boiling point. Simmer 2 minutes and sprinkle with a mixture of 2 tablespoons minced orange peel, 2 tablespoons minced parsley and 2 teaspoons minced garlic.

BAKED PORK CHOPS

Serves 6

1 cup dried apricots
¼ cup maple syrup
½ cup flour
½ teaspoon salt
¼ teaspoon pepper
¼ teaspoon thyme
6 pork chops

Soak the apricots in water for 1 hour with the maple syrup. Mix the flour, salt, pepper and thyme and rub onto both sides of the chops. Sauté the chops in 2 tablespoons butter. Arrange in a baking dish. Place apricots on chops and dot with butter. Bake for 1 hour in moderate oven, 375 degrees. If maple syrup mixture is not all absorbed by apricots, pour over chops.

MARINATED PORK CHOPS

Serves 4

4 thick pork chops
1 cup wine vinegar
1 sprig parsley
1 cup fine bread crumbs
1 clove garlic, pressed
Salt
Pepper
1 egg
1 tablespoon water
½ cup flour
¼ cup oil

Marinate the meat in the vinegar for 1 hour. Chop the parsley. Mix the parsley and bread crumbs together and add the pressed garlic. Season to taste with salt and pepper. Beat the egg with the water. Remove the chops from the vinegar. Sprinkle them with salt and pepper. Roll in flour, dip into the egg and then into the crumbs. Heat the oil. Sauté the chops for about 5 minutes on each side. Lower the heat, cover the pan and continue cooking until the meat is tender, 20 to 25 minutes.

ROAST PORK

Serves 8 to 10

4 to 5 pound pork roast
Lemon juice
Salt
Pepper
Flour
2 cups milk
1 clove garlic

Marinate pork with lemon juice, salt and pepper. Sprinkle with flour. Pour milk over it, adding a clove of garlic to the juices. Cook in a medium oven (350 degrees) 30 minutes to the pound.

CROWN ROAST OF PORK

Serves 8

6 pound crown roast of pork

Stuffing

6 cups fresh bread cubes
3 cups washed cranberries
2 cups chopped, peeled apple
1 cup chopped onion
1 cup chopped celery
1 tablespoon grated orange rind
2 teaspoons cinnamon
1 teaspoon dried rosemary leaves
½ cup butter or margarine, melted

In large bowl combine all ingredients except butter or margarine and toss until very well mixed. Drizzle with the butter until all bread cubes are moistened. Place roast on a square of aluminum foil in shallow roasting pan and fill center with stuffing. Spoon any remaining stuffing in another baking pan. Insert meat thermometer where roast is joined into thickest part of meat. Roast at 350 degrees for 2 hours or until thermometer registers 175 degrees. Bake remaining stuffing, covered, in same oven during second hour of cooking roast. Remove roast on foil to serving platter. Then pull out foil. Spoon extra stuffing around roast.

APPLE CREAM PORK CHOPS

Serves 2

2 (½-inch thick) pork chops
Salt
Pepper
1 large tart apple
½ teaspoon celery salt
Vegetable oil
⅓ cup white wine or dry vermouth
⅓ cup whipping cream

Trim chops of fat. Sprinkle on both sides with salt and black pepper; pound lightly. Spread thinly sliced, quartered apple over bottom of shallow au gratin dish or casserole, 1 to 1½ inches deep. Sprinkle with the celery salt. Brown chops on both sides in very hot vegetable oil. Do not cook chops. Put chops on top of apple; pour in wine. Cover lightly with foil and bake at 350 degrees for 45 minutes. Remove foil, pour the heavy cream over the chops and bake 15 or 20 minutes more.

ROAST LOIN OF PORK WITH BAKED BEANS

Serves 8

1 pound small navy beans
½ teaspoon baking soda
3 to 4 pound pork roast, rubbed with salt, pepper and rosemary
⅔ cup light molasses (golden)
1 tablespoon sugar
2 tablespoons dry mustard
¼ teaspoon black pepper
1 teaspoon salt
1 medium onion, chopped

Soak beans overnight. Drain and add fresh water 1 inch higher than beans and ½ teaspoon baking soda. Parboil for 20 minutes. Drain beans and rinse with cold water and drain once again. Place roast in bottom of 4-quart iron pot or bean pot. Add beans and chopped onion around roast. Mix sugar, molasses, dry mustard, pepper and salt with enough hot water so that ingredients pour easily. Add this mixture to beans with more water so that beans are just covered with liquid. Bake covered in 325 degree oven for 4 hours, periodically adding more water in small amounts to keep beans just moist. Bake uncovered to brown during last 30 to 45 minutes.

Cut glass decanter and "blue and white" soup plate.

SOUTH CAROLINA HOPPIN' JOHN FOR MANY PEOPLE

Serves 16 to 20

3 pounds dried black-eyed peas
4 pounds hog jowl or breakfast bacon, not too lean
4 cups finely chopped onions
1 pound raw rice
2 teaspoons dried ground rosemary
2 teaspoons dry mustard
2 teaspoons hot pepper sauce
1 cup bourbon whiskey
Salt to taste

Soak peas in cold water overnight. Cut jowls or bacon strips into ½-inch square pieces. Brown in large skillet. Remove from heat; let stand at room temperature. Do not pour off grease. Add chopped onions to grease in the skillet; sauté until they are soft. Allow them to remain in grease. Cook rice until it is fluffy and set aside for later use. Pour water off the peas, cover them with fresh water and cook uncovered over low heat until soft (covering the peas while cooking would cause them to "shell out"). In a large container place the rice, peas, hog jowl or bacon. Pour in the onions with all the grease; add rosemary, mustard and hot pepper sauce. Stir the contents, mix it together, stirring only with a large fork so the mixture does not break up but remains whole. Place the contents in 4 large crocks, each crock about 2-quart size. To this point the Hoppin' John may be prepared the day before serving. Set the crocks, uncovered, in a pan of water that comes ½ way up the sides of the crocks. Allow the contents to steam over low heat for 2 hours so the ingredients meld and grease is absorbed. Serve the Hoppin' John in a large container and add the bourbon whiskey.

VEAL SCALLOPS WITH MUSTARD SAUCE

Serves 3 to 4

8 veal scallops, pounded thin (about ¾ pound)
½ cup flour, seasoned with salt and pepper
4 tablespoons butter
2 tablespoons minced shallots
¼ cup dry white wine
½ cup heavy cream
1 tablespoon Dijon mustard

Dredge the scallops in seasoned flour. Heat butter in a large, heavy skillet. Add the scallops and cook quickly until golden brown, approximately 2 minutes a side. Do a few at a time if they are large. Remove scallops to a flat casserole dish and keep warm. Add shallots to skillet and cook briefly, stirring. Add wine and cook, stirring until almost all of the liquid has evaporated. Add cream and let it boil up, stirring. Cook about 30 seconds; then remove from heat. Stir in mustard, season to taste and spoon sauce over meat.

GLORIA'S VEAL TONNATO

Serves 4

1½ pound boneless roast of veal
1 (2 ounce) can anchovy filets
1 medium carrot
1 medium onion
1 stalk celery
1 clove garlic
1 bay leaf
Salt and pepper to taste
1 (3¼ ounce) can tuna fish

Put the veal in a pot and cover with water. Add ½ can anchovies, carrot, onion, celery, garlic, salt, pepper and bay leaf. Boil slowly until meat is tender. Prepare mayonnaise as follows:

Mayonnaise
2 egg yolks
1½ cups good olive oil or corn oil
2 teaspoons capers, chopped
1 teaspoon chopped parsley
¼ teaspoon dry mustard

Place 2 egg yolks in blender; add oil slowly in steady stream until thickened. Add the mustard. Divide mayonnaise in half. To one half add the can of tuna that has been mashed and the rest of the anchovies, parsley and capers. Thinly slice the veal and put on a large platter, slice after slice. Cover with the tuna-anchovy mayonnaise and then cover with the plain mayonnaise. Decorate with sliced hard-boiled eggs or deviled eggs and sliced tomatoes. Serve cold.

SCALLOPINI FLORENTINI

Serves 8

16 pieces veal scallopini, pounded thin
2 cloves garlic, sliced
1¼ teaspoons thyme
Olive oil
½ cup beef stock
1 pound mozzarella cheese, thinly sliced
Salt
Pepper
1½ cups white wine
¼ bay leaf
Small pinch rosemary
8 paper-thin slices prosciutto (or any lean raw ham or Canadian bacon)
3 packages frozen chopped spinach, cooked with a tablespoon or 2 of butter, drained and then pressed dry

Pound the scallopini, season with pepper and soak overnight in a marinade made of white wine, garlic, bay leaf, thyme and rosemary. Drain, reserving marinade. Dry each piece of veal thoroughly (they will not brown if wet). Heat olive oil and brown the veal a few pieces at a time, adding oil as you need it. Set veal aside and brown ham. Set ham aside. In the same frying pan, reduce the strained marinade and the beef stock until slightly thick, scraping the pan. In a casserole, arrange 1 layer of veal slices and top each with a slice of cheese. Cover with the spinach, salt and pepper, then cheese. Now the ham; another layer of cheese and finally the rest of the veal. Pour marinade sauce over and put a bit more cheese on top. It may now wait until about an hour before baking and serving. Bake uncovered at 325 degrees for 1 hour.

...every [one] was his own Cook our Spits was Forked Sticks our Plates was a Large Chip as for Dishes we had none...

from George Washington's Journey
Over the Mountains, 1748

Potomac Harvest

From General Washington's house...I have seen...hundreds, perhaps...thousands of sturgeon, at a great height from the water at the same instant...(Marquis de Chastellux, 1781). The Potomac yielded great quantities of fish which were harvested each spring for use at Mount Vernon and also offered for sale. In 1774 alone, Washington sold more than 1500 barrels of salted fish to two customers in Philadelphia and the West Indies.

(Photograph by Ted Vaughan)

MAUD'S SWEETBREADS IN CREAM SAUCE

Serves 4

1½ pounds veal sweetbreads
2 to 3 stalks celery, with leaves
2 generous sprigs parsley (reserve enough for garnish)

Place sweetbreads in saucepan and cover with cold water. Add celery and parsley. Bring to a boil, then lower heat and simmer for 20 to 25 minutes. Strain, reserving ¼ cup of stock. Place sweetbreads in a bowl of water to cool. Drain well and remove skin and membrane.

Cream Sauce
⅓ cup milk
3 scant tablespoons flour
¼ cup stock
1 cup table cream
½ teaspoon salt
Dash red pepper
1 cup sliced mushrooms
3 tablespoons sherry
Paprika

Add milk gradually to flour to make a smooth paste. Combine this with stock, cream, salt and a dash of red pepper. Add sliced mushrooms which have been sautéed lightly in butter and then gently fold in sweetbreads along with sherry. Place mixture in buttered baking dish and heat in 350 degree oven for 25 to 30 minutes or until hot. Garnish with sprinkle of paprika and chopped parsley.

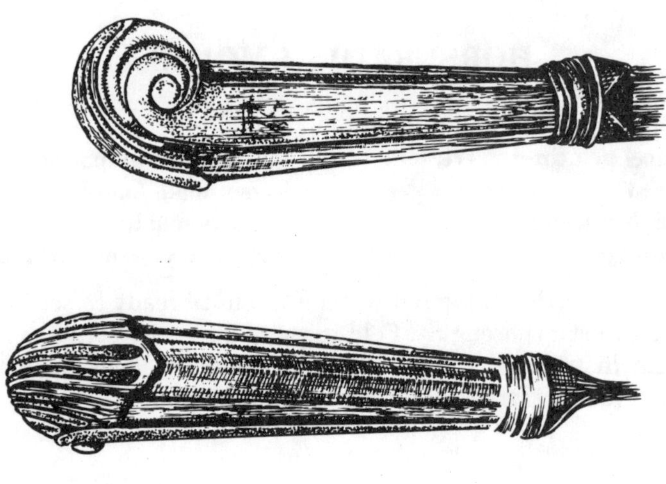

"Pistol handle" flatware.

FREEZER READY CURRY SAUCE

Yield: 4 cups

1 pound bacon, diced
1 cup celery, thinly sliced
1 cup chopped onion
2 garlic cloves, minced
6 tablespoons vegetable oil
4 tablespoons sugar
4 tablespoons lemon juice
8 beef bouillon cubes
1 cup flour
2 cups applesauce
⅓ cup curry powder
12 tablespoons tomato paste
5 cups water
Salt

Sauté bacon until crisp and remove from pan, leaving ⅓ cup fat. Sauté celery, onion and garlic in fat until tender. Sprinkle flour over vegetables and cook, stirring, for 5 minutes. Add applesauce, curry powder, tomato paste, sugar, lemon, bouillon cubes, water, salt and bacon. Cook covered over low heat for 45 minutes. Freeze in 1-cup portions. Add 1 cup milk or light cream *to each 1 cup frozen portion* when ready to use. Heat. Add 2 cups cooked, cubed lamb or chicken, eggs or seafood. Serve over rice.

HORSERADISH MOUSSE

Serves 8

1 (3 ounce) gelatin dessert, lemon flavored
1½ cups hot water
½ cup mayonnaise
6 tablespoons prepared horseradish (one 4-ounce jar)
¼ teaspoon salt
½ cup heavy cream, whipped

Dissolve gelatin dessert in hot water. Chill until ready to set but watch it so you can stir thoroughly. Fold in mayonnaise, horseradish and salt. Then fold in whipped cream. Chill. This can be chilled in a large or individual molds. Serve with roast beef.

Cheese, Eggs & Pasta

The Washingtons' japanned plate warmer.

BAKED EGGS WITH CHEESE

Serves 6

12 eggs
1 to 2 teaspoons dry mustard
1 to 2 teaspoons curry powder
½ to 1 cup mayonnaise
Salt and pepper to taste

Hard boil 12 eggs. Peel shell and cut eggs in half lengthwise. Mash egg yolks, mix with mustard, curry powder, mayonnaise and salt and pepper to taste. Stuff the egg whites and place in buttered shallow dish, 8x13 inches.

Cream Sauce

4 tablespoons flour
4 tablespoons butter
2 cups heated milk
3 drops TABASCO brand pepper sauce
1½ cups shredded sharp Cheddar cheese
6 slices bacon, cooked and crumbled

Make a basic cream sauce by melting butter, adding flour to it and stirring for 1 to 2 minutes. Add heated milk a little at a time until all the milk is added. Add shredded cheese and mix well. Taste for correct seasoning. Pour over top of eggs. Sprinkle top with bacon pieces and bake for 15 minutes at 350 degrees.

BILL'S EGGS

Serves 2 to 4

8 strips bacon
2 tablespoons butter
1 cup cream
4 eggs
Salt
Pepper
Cayenne pepper
4 tablespoons grated cheese
4 slices bread
1 small wine glass sherry

Broil bacon. Melt butter in pan and when melted add the cream. Drop eggs, without breaking the yolks, into pan and sprinkle with salt, pepper and cayenne. When whites are nearly firm, sprinkle with cheese and finish cooking. Toast bread and cover with bacon. Place 1 egg on each square of toast and bacon. To remaining cream mixture, add sherry and pour over eggs.

CREAMED EGG CASSEROLE

Serves 4

3½ tablespoons butter
2 tablespoons flour
½ cup beef broth
½ cup whole milk or half and half
8 or 10 large fresh mushrooms
Salt and pepper to taste
6 large hard-boiled eggs, peeled and sliced
Grated cheese
Cracker crumbs
Paprika

Heat 1½ tablespoons of the butter. Stir in the flour and cook slowly for 2 to 3 minutes without browning. Whisk in the beef broth and milk until smooth. Sauté the mushrooms in 2 tablespoons of butter and add any drippings from the pan in which the mushrooms have been sautéed. Salt and pepper this sauce to taste and cook slowly until thick. Stir in the sliced mushrooms and *very gently* the sliced eggs. Carefully place in a 1-quart casserole, which has been buttered, and sprinkle generously with the grated cheese and cracker crumbs. Dust with paprika. Bake in a 350 degree oven until brown.

SCRAMBLED EGG CASSEROLE

Serves 8

12 slices lean bacon
12 eggs
5 tablespoons milk
1 cup shredded Cheddar cheese
2 tablespoons chopped parsley
1 (8 ounce) carton commercial sour cream
2 teaspoons salt
2 teaspoons pepper

Fry bacon in large skillet, drain and set aside. Add milk to well-beaten eggs and cook in same skillet until firm but still moist. Add 1 cup Cheddar cheese; stir until partially melted. Add sour cream, parsley, salt and pepper. Fold gently until well mixed. Pour mixture into a flat pyrex or foil pan, 9x13 inches. Crumble bacon evenly over top. Bake at 325 degrees for 35 minutes or until hot. *Freezes nicely.*

CHEESE FONDUE

Serves 4

1 cup dry white wine (preferably Rhine)
1 clove garlic, whole, peeled
1 pound Swiss cheese, shredded
1½ tablespoons flour
Salt
Pepper
Nutmeg
3 teaspoons Kirsch
1 loaf French bread, cut into bite-size pieces

In a double boiler heat wine with garlic, until hot. Remove garlic. Dredge cheese with flour. Add cheese to wine, a handful at a time, stirring after each addition until cheese is melted. Season and add Kirsch. Place in a chafing dish and serve with a basket of bread.

MAKE AHEAD CHEESE SOUFFLÉ

Serves 4

6 tablespoons butter
1 tablespoon flour
1 teaspoon salt
Cayenne pepper
Onion salt
Dry mustard
1½ cups milk
10 ounces sharp Cheddar cheese, shredded
6 large cold eggs, separated
Pinch cream of tartar

Preheat oven to 325 degrees. Butter a 2-quart soufflé dish. In a double boiler melt butter and blend in flour, ½ teaspoon salt and the rest of the seasonings to taste, with a wire whisk or a wooden spoon. Gradually stir in cold milk and bring to boil. Stir until smooth and thickened. Reduce heat, add cheese and stir until melted. Remove from heat. Beat egg yolks until thick and lemon colored. Gradually beat cooked mixture into egg yolks. Beat whites with ½ teaspoon salt and a pinch of cream of tartar until very stiff but not dry. With a wire whisk, using an under-and-over motion, gently fold ⅓ of the whites into warm cheese mixture. Carefully fold in remaining egg whites until just combined. Turn into soufflé dish and bake uncovered for 45 minutes or until puffed and golden brown. Do not open the oven door. Serve at once. *Soufflé may be made up ahead and refrigerated as long as 24 hours. Put soufflé in cold oven and bake 50 minutes at 325 degrees. Can also be frozen up to 7 days. Allow 50 to 60 minutes to bake frozen at the same temperature.*

BAKED GNOCCHI

Serves 4 to 6

1 quart milk
¾ cup quick cream of wheat
4 tablespoons butter
2 egg yolks, beaten
¾ cup freshly grated imported Parmesan cheese
Additional grated cheese for top and serving

Heat to scalding 1 quart of milk in top of double boiler. Add cream of wheat in thin stream, stirring with wire whisk. Cook until thick, probably 10 to 15 minutes. Stir frequently to prevent cereal from sticking to bottom of pan. Add butter in 4 pieces. Stir. Add beaten egg yolks and stir. Add grated cheese. Butter an 8x10-inch oven-proof baking dish and fill with cream of wheat mixture. Sprinkle liberally with more cheese and dot with butter. (Can be prepared to this point, covered with plastic wrap and refrigerated, even the day before.) If refrigerated, bring to room temperature and bake in 350 degree oven until nicely browned, 15 minutes to ½ hour. Serve with additional grated cheese.

HOMINY GNOCCHI

Serves 6

1 quart milk
½ cup butter
1 cup hominy grits
1 teaspoon salt
⅓ cup butter, melted
1½ cups grated Parmesan cheese

Scald milk, add butter, stir in grits and sprinkle with salt. Cook, stirring, until thick. Pour into 9x12-inch baking dish. Cook 25 to 30 minutes. When cold, cut into circles with a 1½-inch circle cookie cutter. Place circles in greased oblong oven-proof dish. Pour the melted butter over the gnocchi and sprinkle them with grated cheese. Heat in 350 degree oven until bubbly and lightly browned.

Bearing in grateful remembrance the very fine Cheeses, you had the goodness to send me, Mrs. Washington prays your acceptance of half a dozen Hams of her own curing.

George Washington to William Hambly
July 28, 1798

RICHARD'S FETTUCINE

Serves 4

8 ounces uncooked fettucine noodles, medium width
3 to 4 tablespoons sweet butter
2 eggs
Salt
Pepper
¾ to 1 cup freshly grated imported Parmesan cheese
½ pound bacon, cooked crisp and crumbled

Cook fettucine in large quantity of salted, boiling water. (If the pasta is freshly made, 3 to 4 minutes; if commercial, approximately 8 minutes. In any case until it is *al dente.)* Quickly drain and toss with butter in a heavy hot bowl. Pour beaten eggs in thin stream over pasta, tossing lightly. Add salt and pepper to taste and grated cheese. Fold in crumbled bacon. Serve at once with additional cheese.

GRITS CASSEROLE

Serves 6 to 8

1 cup quick-cooking grits
1 teaspoon salt
4 cups water
8 tablespoons butter
¼ pound processed cheese
¼ pound sharp cheese, shredded
3 eggs, slightly beaten
⅓ cup milk

Cook grits in salted water until done. Then add butter, cheeses, eggs and milk. Stir until melted and smooth. Place in 1½-quart casserole and bake for 1 hour at 325 degrees. Can be made ahead and frozen until ready for use.

JALAPENO CHEESE GRITS

Serves 6

1 cup uncooked grits
4 cups water
4 tablespoons butter
⅓ cup milk
1 (6 ounce) roll Jalapeno cheese
2 eggs, well beaten

Cook grits in water as directed on box. Remove from heat and add butter, milk and cheese. Mix well and let cool slightly. Add eggs. Mix thoroughly. Bake in buttered 1½-quart pyrex casserole for 50 minutes in 325 degree oven.

MUSHROOM AND CHEESE CASSEROLE

Serves 2

3 cups chopped mushrooms
1½ cups bread crumbs
1 cup shredded sharp cheese
4 tablespoons butter
1 tablespoon minced onion
Salt and pepper to taste

Place layer of mushrooms in 1½-quart casserole. Sprinkle with crumbs, then cheese and dot with butter. Add another layer of mushrooms, onion, salt, pepper, crumbs and end with cheese. Cover and bake 20 minutes at 375 degrees. Remove cover for the last few minutes.

POTATO OMELETTE

Serves 6 to 8

4 medium potatoes
4 or 5 eggs
Salt and pepper to taste

Dice potatoes fairly small and fry until cooked and golden in the oil of your choice. Drain potatoes and put in bowl. Beat eggs slightly with salt and pepper; stir into potatoes. Oil a small fairly heavy frying pan and heat. Pour in egg and potato mixture. Cook over medium heat, stirring a bit to allow more of the eggs to set. When there is still a bit of liquid egg left, slide the omelette out onto a plate. Oil the pan again and warm. Invert pan over the plate with omelette and flip it into the pan, uncooked side down. Continue to cook until it is done to your taste. *Other seasonings may be added according to taste—chopped spring onions, fines herbes, anything that you fancy.*

PUFFY QUICHE

Serves 6

3 eggs
½ cup melted butter
½ cup buttermilk biscuit mix
1½ cups milk
¼ teaspoon salt
⅛ teaspoon pepper
¼ teaspoon thyme, summer savory or parsley
⅛ teaspoon garlic powder
½ cup cooked ham or bacon
1 cup shredded cheese

Preheat oven to 350 degrees. Put eggs, butter, biscuit mix, milk, salt, pepper and spices into blender and mix well. Pour into 9-inch pie pan. Sprinkle with meat and then cheese. Press this below surface with back of spoon. Bake for 45 minutes or until cooked.

SAUSAGE STRATA

Serves 6

6 slices bread (no crusts)
1 pound sausage meat, cooked and broken into small pieces
½ pound shredded Swiss cheese
3 eggs, beaten
2 cups half and half
½ teaspoon salt
1 teaspoon Worcestershire sauce
¼ teaspoon nutmeg
Few grinds of pepper

Put bread in a 10x6x1½-inch buttered casserole. Cover with sausage and cheese. Mix eggs, cream, salt, Worcestershire, nutmeg and pepper. Pour over casserole. Let stand several hours. Cook at 350 degrees for 30 minutes.

STANDBY WELSH RAREBIT (ALIBI)

Yield: 1 pound cheese will serve 4 to 6 people

6 pounds natural Cheddar cheese
Beer

Break up cheese (never use processed cheese; it becomes stringy) in small pieces and melt over hot water in a double boiler. Add enough beer to liquify slightly. Serve in a chafing dish. Spread on toast or matzo crackers for a cocktail snack. This keeps for several weeks in the refrigerator. Reheat, adding a little beer if necessary.

BASILICO PESTO

Yield: 1 pint

1 cup finely chopped basil
1 cup finely chopped parsley
1 clove garlic, finely chopped
¾ cup grated Parmesan cheese
1 cup olive oil

The basil, parsley and garlic may be chopped in a food processor. Mix first 4 ingredients thoroughly in a deep jar. Add olive oil a little at a time, stirring constantly until the consistency is pasty. Pour a thin layer of olive oil over the top of the mixture and cover the jar tightly. This will keep several months in the refrigerator. Toss over pasta sparingly.

Vegetables

One of two dipping cisterns in the lower garden.

CHINESE ASPARAGUS

Serves 6 to 8

2 pounds asparagus
6 tablespoons butter
Salt
Pepper
Soy sauce

Cut asparagus into diagonal pieces. Place in a colander and lower into boiling water for 2 minutes. Drain. Toss into a heavy skillet in which you have melted the butter. Toss and season with salt, pepper and a drop of soy sauce.

SWISS ASPARAGUS CASSEROLE

Serves 4 to 6

5 tablespoons butter, divided
2 cups fresh asparagus, sliced diagonally
1 medium onion, sliced
1 tablespoon flour
Salt and pepper to taste
1 cup sour cream
1 cup shredded imported Swiss cheese
¼ cup cracker crumbs

Melt 2 tablespoons butter in large skillet. Sauté asparagus 2 or 3 minutes until barely tender. Remove from pan and set aside. In same skillet sauté onion in 2 tablespoons butter until onion is soft. Stir in flour, salt and pepper. Cook 1 minute until flour is well blended. Add sour cream and shredded cheese. Cook, stirring constantly, over low heat until cheese melts. Spoon asparagus into buttered shallow baking dish. Top with cheese and sour cream mixture. Sprinkle with crumbs and dot with remaining butter. Bake at 400 degrees for 20 minutes. If top is not brown, place under broiler for additional minute or 2.

...The President came and desired us to walk in to dinner...The dinner was very good...peas, lettuce, cucumbers, artichokes, etc....

Amariah Frost's Diary, June 1797

STUFFED BAKED AVOCADOS

Serves 4

2 ripe avocados, halved with shell left on
¼ cup olive oil
2 tablespoons chopped scallions or small green onions
1 (16 ounce) can pear tomatoes, drained and chopped or 1½ cups fresh tomatoes, skinned, squeezed and chopped
4 tablespoons herb stuffing crushed a bit
¼ cup imported Parmesan cheese, grated
2 tablespoons melted butter
½ teaspoon salt
½ teaspoon freshly ground pepper

In a saucepan heat olive oil, add scallions and cook until limp. Stir in tomatoes and simmer approximately 5 minutes or until liquid is somewhat reduced. Add 2 tablespoons of herb crumbs. Brush avocados inside and out with butter. Fill centers with tomato mix and sprinkle tops with crumbs and cheese. Broil 5 to 6 inches from flame or heat until brown on top. Watch carefully! Best eaten with a spoon but salad fork is possible. Good as a vegetable. Delicious as a luncheon dish.

GREEN BEAN CASSEROLE

Serves 4 to 6

2½ cups green string beans
3 tablespoons butter
4 tablespoons flour
½ teaspoon salt
2 cups whole milk
½ cup shredded Cheddar cheese
¼ teaspoon basil
Paprika

Cook and carefully drain the green beans. Place in a greased glass 1-quart casserole baking dish and set aside. Melt the butter and thoroughly mix with the flour, salt and milk. Add the basil. Cook and stir this mixture in a double boiler until thick and smooth. While still hot, stir in the Cheddar cheese. Then pour the cheese sauce over the green beans in the casserole. With a fork, mix lightly. Dust with the paprika. Bake in a 325 degree oven for about 30 minutes.

GREEN BEANS WITH MUSTARD SAUCE

Serves 4

2 pounds fresh green beans or 20 ounces frozen
3 tablespoons sweet butter
3 teaspoons Dijon mustard
½ teaspoon salt
¼ teaspoon white pepper
4 tablespoons wheat germ

Trim beans and cut into 2-inch pieces. Steam beans for 7 minutes, remove from heat and keep warm. Melt butter and stir in mustard, salt and pepper. Stir and cook for 2 minutes over low heat. Drain beans and put in warm serving dish. Pour mustard sauce and wheat germ over beans and toss. Adjust seasoning if necessary.

SNIBBLED BEANS

Serves 6 to 8

2 pounds fresh green string beans, frenched
1 large onion, thinly sliced
6 slices bacon, cooked until crisp and crumbled (reserve ½ of fat in pan)
2 eggs
½ cup cider vinegar
½ cup sugar
Salt to taste

Cook beans in as little water as possible until tender but still crisp (or steam until tender but crisp). Drain and hold, keeping warm. Blend eggs, sugar and vinegar, beating well. Add onions. Pour into skillet with remaining bacon fat and cook over moderate heat, whisking all the while. When thickened, pour over beans. Sprinkle crumbled bacon on top and serve at once. Good with any beef or pork roast.

STRING BEANS WITH ROSEMARY

Serves 4

12 ounces green beans
2 tablespoons butter
1 teaspoon crushed, dried rosemary
Salt and pepper to taste

Snap off ends of beans and remove strings, if any. Soak in ice water for at least 1 hour. Drain and cook in steamer for 5 to 8 minutes, until beans are tender but still crisp and bright green. In a saucepan melt butter, add rosemary and beans and toss lightly. Add salt and freshly ground pepper to taste.

WHITE BEAN CASSEROLE

Serves 8

1 pound dried Great Northern white beans
6 medium onions, sliced
1 cup tomato catsup
⅔ cup brown sugar
½ pound bacon, chopped
Salt to taste
1 teaspoon mustard

Wash beans. Combine with onions in large pan with water to cover. Let stand overnight. Drain. Add fresh water. Cook until tender. Combine sugar, catsup, mustard, bacon and salt in bowl and mix well. Mix in drained beans. Place in baking dish and bake 45 minutes at 325 degrees.

ORANGE BEETS

Serves 6

2 oranges
3 to 4 cups small, whole canned beets
1½ tablespoons butter
2 tablespoons flour
½ teaspoon salt
1 tablespoon honey
2 tablespoons brown sugar
1 tablespoon lemon juice
2 tablespoons cointreau

Remove the orange part of the rind. Squeeze the oranges. You should have 1 cup of juice. Chop the orange peel very fine. Drain the beets. Heat the butter in a small saucepan. Whisk in the flour, salt, honey, sugar, orange and lemon juice and continue whisking until the sauce is thick and smooth. Add the orange peel and beets. Stir carefully and when very hot add the cointreau. These can be eaten hot or cold.

Chinese export salad bowl from the "Cincinnati" service purchased by Washington in 1780.

PURÉED BROCCOLI

Serves 8

3 pounds broccoli
6 tablespoons butter
4 tablespoons minced shallots or onion
4 tablespoons heavy cream (optional)
Pinch nutmeg
Salt and pepper to taste

Cut off flowerets and set aside. Discard tough ends of stalk. Peel rest of stalks and cut them into 1-inch pieces. Cook the stalk pieces in boiling salted water for 8 minutes. Then add the flowerets and cook for 4 minutes more. Drain and then blot broccoli on paper towels. Cook the shallots or onion in 3 tablespoons of butter over low heat until they are transparent. Scrape the pan into a food processor and add the broccoli in batches until all is puréed. Reheat the purée and add the rest of the butter and spices and heavy cream, if desired.

MARRONS AND BRUSSELS SPROUTS

Serves 6

1½ pounds brussels sprouts
¾ pound peeled chestnuts or 1 (15½-ounce) can whole chestnuts in water
2 cups chicken or beef broth
6 tablespoons butter
Freshly grated nutmeg to taste
Salt
Pepper

Trim the sprouts, making an X in the bottom of any large sprouts to insure even cooking. Soak in salted water for 10 minutes. Steam brussels sprouts 5 to 10 minutes until tender crisp. Return to saucepan and shake them dry over moderate heat. At the same time, boil the peeled chestnuts in broth for 15 minutes uncovered. (If using canned chestnuts, drain well and heat in broth.) In a large skillet heat the butter and add the sprouts. Transfer the chestnuts with a slotted spoon to the skillet and quickly boil down the broth until it measures about 2 tablespoonsful. Cook the vegetables for a few minutes over low heat, tossing the pan or stirring gently. Season to taste. Add the reduced broth and serve.

BROCCOLI CASSEROLE

Serves 6 to 8

2 packages frozen chopped broccoli, cooked and drained
2 eggs, beaten
1 cup mayonnaise
1 small onion, cut finely
1 can cream of mushroom soup, not diluted
½ stick butter, melted
1 cup shredded Cheddar cheese
1 cup cheese cracker crumbs

Combine all ingredients, saving ½ of cheese and ½ of cheese cracker crumbs to go on top of casserole. Bake 45 minutes at 350 degrees. *Chopped spinach is also good.*

CABBAGE COOKED IN ORANGE JUICE

Serves 4

½ head medium-size cabbage, shredded coarsely (approximately 3 cups)
2 tablespoons butter
2 tablespoons sugar
½ cup orange juice
1 tablespoon lemon juice
½ teaspoon salt
Freshly ground pepper to taste

Melt butter in 8-inch heavy frying pan (not iron). Add cabbage and all other ingredients. Simmer over low heat to medium heat until done but still crisp, approximately 10 minutes.

CRISP COOKED CABBAGE

Serves 8 to 10

2 pounds cabbage, shredded coarsely
4 tablespoons butter
1 cup half and half
Salt and pepper
1 teaspoon caraway seeds (optional)

Throw the shredded cabbage into a large kettle of boiling salted water. Cook just 12 minutes. Drain and freshen in cold water. Just before serving, reheat the cabbage in a skillet, containing heated butter and cream, tossing with a fork until thoroughly heated. Season with salt and pepper and caraway seeds, if desired.

GERMAN CABBAGE

Serves 6

1 medium cabbage
1 tablespoon vegetable shortening
2 tablespoons finely chopped onion
2 cooking apples, peeled and sliced thin
1 bay leaf
2 to 3 whole cloves
1 teaspoon salt
¼ cup boiling water
2 to 3 tablespoons red wine vinegar
2 tablespoons sugar
Chopped dill weed to taste

Cut cabbage in thin strips. Remove hard core. Wash and drain. In a saucepan, melt shortening and sauté onion for 5 minutes. Add the cabbage, apple slices, bay leaf, cloves, salt and boiling water. Cover and simmer over low heat for ½ hour. Add red wine vinegar and sugar and simmer 10 minutes longer. Taste and add more vinegar and sugar if necessary. Just before serving, season with dill weed.

SAVORY CABBAGE

Serves 6

1 medium-sized cabbage
4 tablespoons butter
1 medium-sized onion, chopped
½ pint light cream or milk
Salt and pepper to taste

Chop cabbage medium fine. Melt butter in frying pan. Sauté cabbage, onions, salt and pepper until both cabbage and onions are soft. Add cream to cabbage mixture and simmer, covered, for 20 minutes on top of stove. For a less rich dish, milk may be substituted.

CARROT FRITTERS

Yield: 36 fritters or 6 servings

1 cup flour
1 teaspoon baking powder
1 egg
1 tablespoon sugar
1 lemon, squeezed
1 cup cooked carrots, mashed
1 quart frying oil
¼ cup powdered sugar

Mix together flour, baking powder, egg, granulated sugar, lemon juice and carrots. Heat oil to 375 degrees in a deep fat fryer. Drop mixture by teaspoonful into the hot oil and cook until golden brown. Drain, sprinkle with powdered sugar and serve.

CARROT CASSEROLE

Serves 6 to 8

12 medium carrots, pared and sliced
1 small onion, minced
¼ cup margarine or butter
¼ cup flour
1 teaspoon salt
¼ teaspoon dry mustard
2 cups milk
⅛ teaspoon pepper
¼ teaspoon celery salt
½ pound mild Cheddar cheese, sliced
1 to 1¼ cups buttered fresh bread crumbs

Cook carrots until tender. In saucepan, gently cook onion in butter for 2 or 3 minutes. Stir in flour, salt, dry mustard, then milk. Cook, stirring, until smooth. Add pepper and celery salt. In a 2-quart casserole alternate layers of carrots and cheese. Pour on sauce and top with crumbs. Bake at 350 degrees for 35 to 40 minutes. This freezes well.

CARROT RING

Serves 10

2 slices bread
3 pounds carrots, sliced
3 tablespoons butter
1 onion, sliced
6 eggs
8 sprigs parsley
2 teaspoons salt
½ teaspoon pepper
2 tablespoons brown sugar
Peas

Make soft crumbs of bread by putting in blender. Set aside. Cook carrots and onion in butter until soft. Blend eggs, parsley, salt, pepper and sugar. Add bread crumbs, carrots and onions. Mix well. Put in buttered 3-cup mold. Cover with foil, put in pan of water and cook at 375 degrees for 30 to 45 minutes. Turn out on platter and fill center with cooked peas.

CORN FRITTERS

Serves 10

12 ears fresh corn
3 eggs, separated
1 teaspoon salt
2 tablespoons flour
2 tablespoons butter

Grate 12 ears of corn. Beat yolks of 3 eggs and add 2 tablespoons of flour, beating well after addition. Beat the whites of the eggs until stiff. Mix the grated corn and the egg yolk mixture. Fold in the beaten whites. Melt 2 tablespoons of butter in skillet and, when hot, drop fritter mixture by tablespoon. When edges are brown, turn and brown on other side. Serve immediately. May be served with maple syrup.

CORN SOUFFLÉ

Serves 6

2 cups cooked corn, cut from cob, or 1 #2 can cream-style corn
1 teaspoon salt
1 tablespoon sugar
2 cups half and half
1 tablespoon cornstarch
4 eggs
4 tablespoons melted butter

Place all ingredients in food processor. Blend for 30 to 60 seconds with on/off switch. Strain (to eliminate hulls) into buttered medium-size soufflé dish and bake 45 minutes in a 375 degree to 400 degree oven. Serve at once.

GREAT GRANDMOTHER'S CORN PUDDING

Serves 6

1 dozen ears corn
1 pint heavy cream
1 tablespoon sugar
1 teaspoon pepper
2 teaspoons salt
Butter

Score and cut corn kernels from cob. Place first 5 ingredients in well-buttered casserole. Dot heavily with butter. Place casserole in pan of water and bake for 45 to 60 minutes in preheated 300 degree oven. Pudding should be nicely brown and firm when tested with knife (as with custard).

QUICK CORN PUDDING

Serves 4

2 eggs
2 heaping teaspoons flour
3 tablespoons strained honey
1 cup half and half
1 (10 ounce) box frozen golden kernel cut corn
Butter
Paprika
Finely chopped parsley

Preheat oven to 325 degrees. In a bowl beat eggs and add flour slowly. Then add honey and half and half while continuing to beat. Fold corn into mixture and pour into 1½-pint greased baking dish. Top with dots of butter and sprinkle lightly with paprika. Set in a shallow pan of water and bake for 35 to 45 minutes. Remove and garnish with parsley before serving.

EGGPLANT CASSEROLE

Serves 6 to 8

2 medium eggplants, peeled and cubed (2 to 3 pounds)
2 cups chopped onions
1 (28 ounce) can tomatoes, well drained and chopped (save juice)
1 teaspoon salt
½ teaspoon pepper
2 tablespoons Worcestershire sauce
½ cup thick cream sauce (see receipt below)
¼ cup plus 1 tablespoon butter
¼ cup bread crumbs
½ cup shredded Cheddar cheese
Paprika

Place eggplant and onions in large pan with water barely to cover. Simmer until tender 5 to 7 minutes. Drain. Add tomatoes, salt, pepper, Worcestershire sauce, cream sauce and ¼ cup butter. Melt remaining tablespoon butter in an 8-cup baking dish; sprinkle bottom with ¼ cup bread crumbs. Add eggplant mixture. Sprinkle top with cheese, remaining crumbs and paprika. Bake at 350 degrees for 10 to 15 minutes or until heated through.

Cream Sauce (very thick)
1½ tablespoons butter
2 tablespoons flour
½ cup juice from tomatoes or milk

In saucepan, melt butter over medium heat and whisk in flour. Slowly add juice or milk, whisking constantly, about 5 minutes.

FLUFFY EGGPLANT

Serves 4

3 cups cooked mashed eggplant
1 cup soda cracker crumbs
¼ cup butter
¾ cup cream
¼ teaspoon ground black pepper

Cut unpeeled eggplant in pieces and boil in water until soft. Mix eggplant with ¾ cup of cracker crumbs. Add melted butter, cream and pepper. Toss lightly with fork. Place in 1-quart casserole. Sprinkle remaining cracker crumbs over top. Dot with butter. Bake 30 minutes in 350 degree oven. *Make ahead of time. Let it stand to improve the flavor.*

EASY EGGPLANT PIE

Serves 4 to 6

Unbaked 9-inch pie shell
4 cups unpeeled and cubed eggplant
¼ cup butter or margarine
½ cup finely chopped onion
1 clove garlic, minced
1 tablespoon chopped parsley
¼ cup chopped celery tops
½ teaspoon salt
¼ teaspoon oregano
⅛ teaspoon pepper
1 (8 ounce) can tomato sauce
½ cup shredded mozzarella cheese

Place eggplant, washed and cut in ½-inch cubes, in melted butter in heavy skillet. Cover and cook over medium heat for 5 minutes. Remove eggplant from skillet with slotted spoon. Cook onion and garlic in skillet, stirring until onion is transparent. Add parsley, celery tops, seasonings and tomato sauce. Cook over medium heat for 5 minutes, stirring constantly. Add eggplant to ingredients. Stir. Partially cool all ingredients. Turn into pie shell. Bake in moderate (350 degree) oven 45 minutes. Sprinkle cheese over top and return to oven a few minutes until cheese melts. Let stand 5 minutes before serving.

EGGPLANT RAMEKINS

Serves 6

3 medium eggplants
6 tomatoes
2 tablespoons butter
1 onion
2 cloves garlic
Thyme to taste
Salt to taste
Pepper to taste
2 pots (5 fluid ounces) sour cream

Slice eggplant and fry slices in oil until golden brown. Line buttered ramekins with slices. Peel, halve and seed the tomatoes. Chop coarsely. Heat the butter and sauté with chopped onion, thyme and crushed garlic until onion is soft. Season with salt and pepper. Put into 6 individual ramekins with alternate layers of tomatoes and sour cream. Top pots with eggplant slices. Cook in a Bain Marie for 25 minutes until cream has set. Leave until cold and turn out. Serve as a luncheon dish or first course.

EASY SPICED EGGPLANT

Serves 4

½ cup olive oil
3 cloves garlic, mashed
1 onion, chopped
1 green pepper, chopped
1 teaspoon powdered coriander
1 teaspoon turmeric
1 teaspoon cumin
1 teaspoon powdered ginger
1 medium eggplant, peeled and cut into ¾-inch cubes
3 to 4 tomatoes, chopped
1 tablespoon brown sugar

Preheat oven to 375 degrees. Cook garlic, onion, pepper, coriander, turmeric, cumin and powdered ginger in olive oil slowly for 10 minutes until onion is translucent. Add eggplant, tomatoes and brown sugar and place in buttered casserole. Cook 1 hour at 375 degrees.

BAKED MUSHROOMS

Serves 6 to 8

2 pounds large mushrooms
3 tablespoons butter
¾ teaspoon salt
¼ teaspoon pepper
¼ teaspoon fines herbs
1 tablespoon lemon juice
1 cup heavy cream

Preheat oven to 350 degrees. Remove stems from mushrooms and dry well. Combine other ingredients. Arrange mushrooms, cavity side up, in a shallow baking pan, dot with butter and pour the cream mixture over top. Bake 20 minutes or until tender.

BRAISED ONIONS

Serves 4 to 6

1½ pounds small white onions or 1 bag frozen pearl onions
2 tablespoons butter
1¼ cup chicken stock
¼ cup sugar
Salt and pepper to taste

Peel fresh onions. Melt butter in saucepan; add the onions and all other ingredients. Cook slowly over a medium-low flame, turning onions occasionally until tender. The liquid should be greatly reduced and beginning to thicken and turn slightly brown.
If using frozen onions use only ½ cup chicken stock.

BAKED ONIONS WITH PECANS

Serves 8

4 large yellow onions, peeled and halved crosswise
1 cup chicken broth
1 tablespoon butter
2 teaspoons honey
1 teaspoon grated lemon rind
¼ teaspoon sweet paprika
¼ cup finely chopped pecans

Arrange onions cut side up in a large greased baking dish in 1 layer. In a saucepan combine chicken broth, butter, honey, lemon rind and sweet paprika and bring mixture to a simmer. Pour mixture over onions and bake the onions, covered, in a preheated 350 degree oven for approximately 1 hour until they are tender to a fork. Remove cover and sprinkle the onions with chopped pecans and brown them lightly under the broiler.

MARY GENE'S ONIONS WITH CHEESE

Serves 6 to 8

1 tablespoon butter
9 to 10 medium yellow onions, sliced thin
4 to 5 slices buttered toast, no crusts
½ pound medium sharp Cheddar cheese, shredded
1 egg
1 cup whole milk
1 teaspoon salt
Freshly ground pepper
1 teaspoon celery seeds

Butter a flat shallow 2-quart baking dish. Boil onions in water to cover until just tender. Drain. Line bottom of dish with toast, cover with layer of onions, then ⅓ of the grated cheese. Repeat until you have 3 layers, ending with onions. At this point casserole may be covered with plastic wrap and refrigerated for several hours. When ready to bake, heat oven to 375 degrees. Beat egg lightly and add milk and seasonings. Pour over contents of casserole, which has been allowed to come to room temperature. Bake for 40 minutes and serve at ounce. Excellent with roast beef, lamb or steak.

PURÉED PARSNIPS

Serves 6

3 pounds parsnips
1 teaspoon salt
1 teaspoon sugar
1 stick (½ cup) melted butter
4 tablespoons heavy cream
Madeira to taste
Buttered bread crumbs

Preheat oven to 350 degrees. Scrub parsnips. Boil in salted water, covered, until tender. The time depends on the age and size of the parsnips. Drain and dip in ice water to make them easier to peel. Peel and cut into pieces and put in blender with all other ingredients except bread crumbs. Spoon purée into 1-quart baking dish. Sprinkle with buttered bread crumbs and bake for 30 minutes.

PARSNIP FRITTERS

Serves 4

4 medium parsnips (1 pound)
2 tablespoons butter
1 teaspoon salt
Dash pepper
2 tablespoons milk
3 tablespoons flour
2 tablespoons drippings

Wash parsnips and cook in a little water until tender, about 30 minutes. Cool and peel; remove center core if tough and woody. Mash thoroughly or force through chopper or ricer into a bowl. Add butter, salt, pepper and milk. Shape into 8 cakes, dip in flour and brown slowly in hot drippings in a heavy skillet.

CHEESE AU GRATIN POTATOES

Serves 8

6 medium size potatoes
6 tablespoons butter
6 tablespoons flour
1 pint half and half
1 cup concentrated chicken broth
1 cup grated Cheddar cheese
Salt
White pepper
Dry bread crumbs
Parmesan cheese

Peel the potatoes and cook in boiling salted water just until tender. Drain and cool while making the sauce. Heat the butter in a small saucepan. Whisk in the flour. Lower the heat and cover. Let the mixture cook 2 to 3 minutes without browning. Whisk in the half and half and the chicken broth and continue whisking until smooth. Add the Cheddar cheese and whisk until the cheese melts. Remove from the heat and season to taste with salt and white pepper. Butter a shallow oven-proof serving casserole. Slice the potatoes ⅓ inch thick and arrange them in the casserole. Pour over the sauce. (All this can be done in advance.) Forty-five minutes before serving, place in a 350 degree oven. Five minutes before the end of cooking time, sprinkle with dry bread crumbs and a little Parmesan cheese.

PEAS AND WATERCRESS RAPPAHANNOCK

Serves 2

1 package frozen peas
1 bunch watercress
2 cubes concentrated chicken bouillon
¾ cup water
Salt and pepper to taste
½ teaspoon lemon juice (optional)

Heat water until boiling in medium size pot. Add chicken cubes and dissolve. Add frozen peas, top with watercress, cover and cook only until watercress wilts. Remove from fire. Drain, reserving liquid. Put pea/watercress combination in a food processor and purée until consistency of Cream of Wheat (not consistency of baby food), adding reserved liquid as necessary. Season with salt and pepper to taste and add lemon juice, if desired. Just before serving put a dollop of butter on top.

POMMES DUCHESSE

Potatoes
Butter
Eggs
Salt
White pepper
Nutmeg

Peel big potatoes and half cook them in salted water. When they are cooked, dry them in the oven and mash into a purée, adding only butter and whole eggs (2 whole eggs for 4 or 5 potatoes). Season with salt, white pepper and a pinch of nutmeg. Fill up a pastry bag with the purée and squeeze onto a buttered sheet, making roses or tress-shaped mounds. Brush them with an egg yolk and brown them in the oven.

RICE PILAF WITH PIGNOLIA AND PISTACHIO NUTS

Serves 6 to 8

2 cups rice
3 tablespoons butter
¼ cup pignolia nuts
¼ cup blanched pistachio nuts, unsalted
1 to 2 teaspoons mace

Cook the rice in boiling salted water for 12 minutes. Drain and rinse in cold water. Drain thoroughly. Melt butter in heavy frying pan over low heat; add pignolia nuts and lightly shake pan until nuts are the color of a popcorn kernel. Add rice. Add pistachio nuts; sprinkle with mace to taste. Cook over low heat until rice is heated.

CURRIED RICE AND FRUIT

Serves 8

¼ cup butter or margarine
⅔ cup chopped onion
4½ cups cooked rice
1½ cups chicken broth
1 teaspoon curry powder
¾ teaspoon salt
¾ teaspoon cinnamon
1 tablespoon grated orange rind
1½ cups peeled, diced apples
1 cup seedless raisins

Melt butter. Add onion and cook until soft. Add rice and broth, curry powder, salt, cinnamon, orange rind, apples and raisins. Mix well and bring to a boil. Put in 2-quart casserole. Cover. (Can be made ahead up to this point.) To serve, put in 350 degree oven and heat 30 minutes. Good with chicken, ham or pork.

PARSLEY RICE SOUFFLÉ

Serves 6 to 8

2 cups cooked rice
¼ pound American cheese, finely shredded
1 teaspoon melted butter
2 eggs, separated
1 cup milk
⅛ teaspoon paprika
Pinch cayenne pepper
1 teaspoon Worcestershire sauce
1 cup finely chopped onion
1 cup chopped parsley

Combine rice, cheese, melted butter, chopped onion, parsley and seasonings. Beat egg yolks and mix with milk; combine with rice mixture. Beat egg whites until stiff. Fold egg whites into rice mixture. Bake in buttered casserole in 350 degree oven for 25 minutes.

SPINACH RING WITH COOKED CUCUMBERS AND HOLLANDAISE SAUCE

Serves 8

6 packages frozen chopped spinach
1 (8 ounce) can water chestnuts, chopped
5 medium-size cucumbers
Never Fail Hollandaise Sauce

Cook (steam preferably) the spinach. Drain *thoroughly,* then add the water chestnuts. Season to taste with salt, pepper, nutmeg or, if unable to use salt, lemon juice. Grease a medium-size ring mold; pack in spinach. This may be done ahead and reheated, covered, in a moderate oven. Prepare the cucumbers by peeling and halving them. Scoop out all the seeds and cut the cucumbers into bite size. Do not overcook (steam preferably) and drain thoroughly.

Hollandaise Sauce
6 egg yolks
⅔ cup water
Juice of 1 lemon
8 tablespoons butter or margarine

Put egg yolks, water and juice of lemon over hot water in a double boiler. Let it thicken, stirring with a wire whisk occasionally. When thick, add the butter and stir *constantly* until it is melted. The sauce is then completed and must IMMEDIATELY be removed from hot water. Refill the bottom of the double boiler with *cold water.* The sauce will stand for hours without separating. Cover until serving time. Slowly reheat, stir again and serve warm, not hot.

To serve:
Unmold the spinach ring onto a warm platter. Fill center with piping hot cucumbers and cover the cucumbers with hollandaise sauce.

BUTTERNUT SQUASH PURÉE WITH THYME

Serves 4

2-pound butternut squash
4 tablespoons unsalted butter
2 tablespoons honey
1½ teaspoons dried thyme
Salt and pepper to taste

Cut squash in half; place cut side down on a greased baking sheet and bake it in a 400 degree oven for approximately 45 minutes or until it pierces easily with a kitchen fork. Turn squash over and let it cool enough to handle. Remove seeds and discard. Scoop out the pulp and place in a food processor fitted with the steel blade. Add 4 tablespoons unsalted butter, cut in pieces, 2 tablespoons honey, 1½ teaspoons dried thyme and, if desired, salt and pepper. Process until smooth and completely mixed, about 30 seconds. Place mixture in a small buttered baking dish and heat in a 400 degree oven for 20 minutes until slightly bubbly.

SUMMER SQUASH OR ZUCCHINI CASSEROLE

Serves 8

3 pounds squash
2 eggs, beaten
6 ounces melted margarine
½ cup milk
½ medium onion, grated
½ teaspoon Worcestershire sauce
2 tablespoons brown sugar
1 teaspoon salt
1 tablespoon chopped parsley
1 cup shredded Cheddar cheese
2½ cups torn bread, crusts removed
Butter or margarine
Paprika

Cook squash, drain well and mash. Add eggs, margarine, milk, onion, Worcestershire, sugar, salt, parsley and cheese. Butter a 3-quart casserole. Put layer of bread, layer of squash mixture 2 times, ending with layer of bread on top. Dot with margarine and sprinkle with paprika. Bake uncovered at 350 degrees for 45 minutes.

EASY ZUCCHINI CASSEROLE

Serves 5 to 6

2 pounds small zucchini
3 to 6 scallions or green onions
3 tablespoons finely chopped dill weed
4 ounces butter
Salt and pepper to taste

Cut zucchini in half lengthwise and then across in pieces ¼ inch thick, or they may be julienned. Chop scallions fine, including green part. Melt butter in baking dish. Toss all ingredients in the butter and cook at 350 degrees, covered, for 35 to 45 minutes. Zucchini should still be a bit crisp.

ZUCCHINI PANCAKES

Serves 8

1¾ pounds zucchini
1 tablespoon salt
3 large eggs, beaten
¾ cup flour
1½ teaspoons baking powder
2 tablespoons butter, or more, as needed, for frying the pancakes

Scrub the zucchini but do not peel them. Trim the ends and put them through the coarse grating blade of a food processor. Turn the grated zucchini into a bowl, add the salt and mix. Set aside for 20 minutes, so that the zucchini will render its liquid. Turn the zucchini into a colander and taste it. If it is very salty, rinse with cold water. Drain well and squeeze dry. Add the drained zucchini to the eggs in a bowl and sift into the mixture the flour and the baking powder. Stir and mix well. Heat the butter in a frying pan over moderately high heat. Use a tablespoon and drop the zucchini mixture into the hot butter. Fry until brown on 1 side, turn the pancakes over and fry until brown on the other side. These pancakes are best served hot but are also delicious cold.

SHREDDED ZUCCHINI

Serves 4

6 zucchini squash
3 tablespoons butter
Salt and seasonings to taste
½ teaspoon grated lemon rind

Shred 6 unpeeled zucchini squash in food processor. Salt generously and place in colander for 15 minutes. Rinse, squeeze fluid from zucchini and sauté in 3 tablespoons of melted butter for 5 minutes. Adjust seasonings; add salt if necessary. Sprinkle with ½ teaspoon grated lemon rind and serve.

XIMENA'S ZUCCHINI TEMPURA

Serves 4

3 medium-sized zucchini
½ cup flour
½ cup beer, very cold
1 cup cooking oil

Slice zucchini crosswise into thin slices. Make a batter of flour and enough beer to make a medium-thin batter, approximately ½ cup of very cold beer. Heat oil in frying pan, dip zucchini slices in batter and deep fry in hot oil for 2 to 3 minutes or until slightly browned. Remove and place on paper towel to dry.

SWEET POTATO-APPLE SOUFFLÉ

Serves 6 to 8

2 tablespoons sugar
1 teaspoon cinnamon
2 cups applesauce
1 tablespoon grated orange rind
3 cups cooked, mashed sweet potatoes
¾ teaspoon salt
⅓ cup melted butter
4 eggs, separated

Combine sugar and cinnamon. Add to applesauce with orange rind. Mix well. Combine sweet potatoes, salt, applesauce mixture and butter. Add beaten egg yolks. Beat egg whites stiff and fold into applesauce-sweet potato mixture. Pile lightly into greased 3-quart casserole. Bake in 400 degree oven for 45 minutes. Serve immediately.

The Lower Garden

Lettuce and beans prosper in the lower garden at Mount Vernon, in beds bordered with herbs, including chives, the purple flower in the center. Pear trees, trained to grow along a fence in a technique known as espalier, can be seen against the wall, with roofs of the south lane outbuildings and mansion in the background. Eighteenth century visitors frequently commented on the estate's neat, well-tended gardens, which supplied fruits and vegetables for the Washingtons' table.

(Photograph by Paul Kennedy)

SWEET POTATO AND ORANGE CASSEROLE

Serves 10

10 sweet potatoes
3 oranges
⅔ cup brown sugar
½ cup butter
1 cup orange juice
½ cup strained honey
Fine bread crumbs

Boil sweet potatoes until almost tender. Arrange layer of sliced potatoes in bottom of casserole. Sprinkle with brown sugar, dot with butter and cover with layer of thinly sliced oranges with skin left on. Repeat layers until ingredients are used. Pour over orange juice mixed with honey. Cover top with brown sugar mixed with fine bread crumbs. Dot with butter. Bake in 350 degree oven for 1 hour.

TOMATOES ALBERT

Serves 6

6 medium-sized ripe tomatoes
2 tablespoons mayonnaise
2 to 4 teaspoons curry powder
2 tablespoons capers
3 tablespoons fine bread crumbs
Dash cayenne pepper (optional)

Topping
Coarse bread crumbs
Finely grated Romano cheese (or pecorino cheese)
Unsalted butter

Cut off top quarter of tomatoes. Scoop out the seeds and center pulp. Mix mayonnaise, curry powder, capers, fine bread crumbs and cayenne pepper. Stuff each tomato with mayonnaise mixture. Top each tomato with coarse bread crumbs; layer on finely grated Romano (or pecorino) cheese and top this with slab of unsalted butter. Place tomatoes in oven-proof baking dish and store in cool place until ready to serve. Place under broiler for 5 minutes or until tops are nicely browned and tomatoes are warm throughout.

CHERRY TOMATOES WITH RUM

Serves 4

1 pint cherry tomatoes
2 tablespoons butter
2 tablespoons light brown sugar
3 tablespoons light rum
1 teaspoon crushed basil
Salt
Pepper
3 tablespoons chopped parsley

Melt butter over medium heat in heavy frying pan. Add brown sugar and blend with butter. Add tomatoes and poach in this sauce for approximately 5 minutes, being careful not to break the skins. Add rum and basil. Cook an additional 2 to 3 minutes. Put into hot vegetable dish, sprinkle with chopped parsley and serve at once.

FRIED GREEN TOMATOES

Serves 6

6 green tomatoes, sliced into ⅓-inch to ½-inch slices
1 cup flour, seasoned with salt, pepper and basil
Bacon drippings or oil

Dip tomato slices in seasoned flour and fry in fat or oil until browned. Do not cook until they get mushy.

FRIED TOMATOES

Serves 6

4 ripe tomatoes, sliced ⅜ inch thick
½ cup flour
2 tablespoons butter
1 tablespoon olive oil
¼ cup heavy cream
Salt and pepper

Dredge tomatoes in the flour, which has a touch of salt in it. Melt butter and oil in a sauté pan and add tomatoes and fry over high heat for 5 minutes or until brown. Turn and brown on other side. Remove to a warm platter. Pour cream into hot pan and scrape all the bits and pieces and pour over the tomatoes. Season to taste.

TURNIPS AND ONIONS

Serves 4 to 6

16 small turnips, peeled
1 medium onion, minced
4 tablespoons butter
1½ teaspoons sugar
Salt
White pepper
¼ cup chicken stock

Parboil the turnips in salted water for 15 minutes. Drain and put in a frying pan with the minced onion and butter. Sprinkle with sugar, salt and white pepper. Sauté until brown, shaking from time to time over a bright flame, about 20 minutes. Deglaze the pan with the chicken stock and pour over the turnips.

TWEED ROOTS

Serves 4 to 6

½ pound carrots
¼ pound parsnips
1 pound potatoes
¼ pound rutabagas
¼ pound turnips
2 cups chicken stock (double strength)
½ cup unsalted butter
Salt and pepper to taste

Peel all vegetables and cut large ones into smaller pieces. Submerge in chicken stock (more may be necessary; canned chicken broth is very satisfactory) and boil until very tender. Drain broth and boil until reduced to ½ cup. Return vegetables to stock and reheat. Then blend very lightly so that mixed root vegetables resemble tweed, i.e., they are very thoroughly mixed but not puréed into baby pap. This can be done with a fork, a hand-powered potato mashing implement or a judiciously light touch on an electric mixer. Just before serving, cut butter into 8 small pieces and stir rapidly into hot mixture. Taste for seasoning (salt and pepper). Remember, canned chicken broth is extremely salty and will likely suffice. *Proportions of various vegetables are approximate. Mixture is better if all 5 roots are used but parsnips and rutabagas should be "minority stock" and too many carrots make color too "high." This can be made in advance. The easiest way to reheat is in a microwave oven. If you must use range top, be careful lest starch sticks.*

FRANCIE'S VEGETABLE PIE

Serves 6 to 8

Pie Shell

1 egg, beaten
2 onions, chopped and lightly sautéed
2 cups cooked rice
Butter

Preheat oven to 350 degrees. Mix beaten egg with sautéed onion and 2 cups of cooked rice. Press into a buttered 9-inch pie plate.

Vegetable Filling

4 cups combined raw, sliced vegetables, using what you might have in the refrigerator —carrots, celery, mushrooms, zucchini, summer squash, green beans, broccoli, cauliflower, etc.
2 tablespoons olive oil
2 tablespoons butter
Salt, pepper and curry powder to taste

Sauté the sliced vegetable combination in the olive oil and butter. Add salt, pepper and curry powder to taste. Place sautéed vegetables into rice shell.

Cheese Topping

¼ cup butter
¼ cup flour
1 cup milk
1 cup shredded Cheddar cheese
1 teaspoon dry mustard powder
Dash cayenne pepper or paprika
Parsley

Melt butter in pan and add flour. Mix well. Slowly stir in milk. Add cheese and stir. Add mustard and paprika or cayenne pepper. Salt and pepper to taste. Top vegetable pie with this mixture. Sprinkle with parsley. Bake in oven 30 minutes.

TURNIP PUFF

Serves 8 to 10

6 to 8 medium white turnips
2 tablespoons butter
1 teaspoon salt
Dash pepper
2 teaspoons sugar
½ teaspoon flour
3 eggs, separated

Peel the turnips and cut into cubes. Cook until soft in boiling water. Drain. Mash well over low heat to dry out excess moisture. Add butter, salt, pepper, sugar and flour. Beat egg whites until stiff. With same beater, beat egg yolks until light. Add yolks to turnip mixture, then fold in egg whites. Pour into buttered 1½-quart oven casserole. Bake uncovered at 350 degrees for 30 to 35 minutes until puffy and lightly browned.

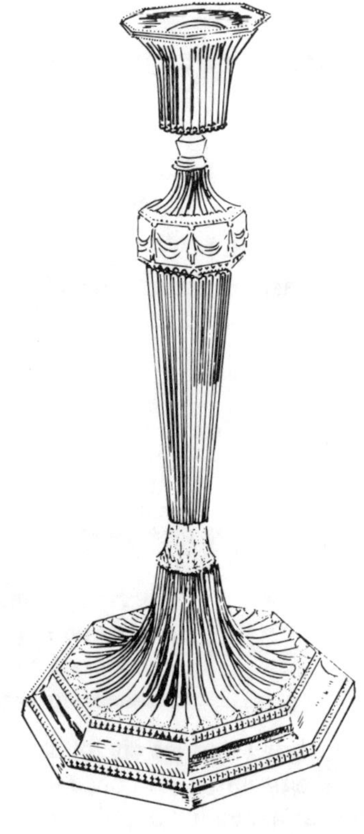

Silver plated candlestick, possibly part of set of eight ordered by George Washington in 1783.

HOLLANDAISE SAUCE

¼ pound butter
2 egg yolks
1 tablespoon lemon juice
Salt and cayenne pepper to taste

Divide butter in thirds and put in bowl of ice. Put enough water in bottom part of double boiler so that it is not touching top part of double boiler. Bring water to a gentle boil. In top of double boiler mix egg yolks and lemon juice. Spear ⅓ of butter with a fork and swish it around in the lemon-egg mixture until melted. Immediately spear another ⅓ of butter and repeat until all butter is melted. Remove from stove, season and serve. Frozen butter can be used.

MUSTARD SAUCE FOR HOT VEGETABLES

Yield: 2 cups

¾ cup mayonnaise
3 tablespoons lemon juice
1½ tablespoons Dijon mustard
½ cup heavy cream, whipped

Mix first 3 ingredients and fold in whipped cream. Serve with hot vegetables such as broccoli, asparagus, beans, etc.

MARIA'S BEER BATTER FOR EGGPLANT

1 (12 ounce) can beer
1 cup flour
½ cup sugar
¼ teaspoon garlic salt
¼ teaspoon onion salt
¼ teaspoon crushed oregano
¼ teaspoon poultry seasoning
¼ teaspoon tarragon

Mix all ingredients in large bowl and let sit for 1 to 3 hours. Heat deep fat to 375 degrees. Peel big eggplants and slice in thin rounds or sticks. Dip in batter and fry a few at a time until golden. Drain on paper towels and keep warm until all slices are cooked. For tiny eggplants, do not peel. Slice very thin almost all the way to the stem so that they open in a fan shape. Then proceed as above. *This batter can be used for other vegetables like zucchini or onions.*

Salads & Salad Dressings

Silver cruet stand with the Washington coat-of-arms ordered from London in 1757.

STUFFED ARTICHOKE SALAD

Serves 6

6 large artichokes
6 hard-boiled eggs
6 tablespoons mayonnaise
Salt to taste
Pepper to taste
TABASCO brand pepper sauce to taste
6 tablespoons minced celery
6 tablespoons chopped olives
6 tablespoons crabmeat or shrimp, chopped

Soak artichokes in cold salted water for 30 minutes. Rinse. Boil in salted water 45 minutes or until tender. To test, pull leaf from middle of artichoke and taste. Remove from water and drain. Chill. Mash eggs and mix with mayonnaise, salt, pepper, Tabasco, celery, olives and crabmeat or shrimp. Remove choke from artichoke as follow: Stand artichoke in small bowl. Open leaves and pull out center leaf carefully, using small sharp spoon. Add edible part from center to egg mixture. Fill artichoke with mixture and serve on lettuce topped with mayonnaise.

MOLDED AVOCADO RING

Serves 10

2 envelopes unflavored gelatin
½ cup fresh grapefruit juice
1¼ cups boiling water
3 cups mashed avocado
⅓ cup lime juice
1 tablespoon sugar
2 tablespoons salt
1 onion, grated
¼ tablespoon TABASCO brand pepper sauce
¾ cup mayonnaise
Pomegranate seeds for decoration

Soak the gelatin in the fresh grapefruit juice and dissolve in boiling water. Blend avocado with lime juice, sugar, salt, grated onion, Tabasco and mayonnaise. Add gelatin. Mix and chill in an 8-cup ring mold. To serve, unmold on a lettuce leaf lined serving platter. Fill the center with shrimp and chopped parsley. Sprinkle the avocado ring with pomegranate seeds.

CRUNCHY CAULIFLOWER SALAD

Serves 8 to 10

1 medium head cauliflower
1 cup sliced radishes
½ cup sliced green onions
1 (8 ounce) can sliced water chestnuts
¾ cup sour cream
¾ cup mayonnaise
2 tablespoons caraway seeds
1 small packet buttermilk salad dressing mix

Cut cauliflower into small flowerets and combine with radishes, green onions and water chestnuts. Stir remaining ingredients together; pour over vegetables. Toss well. Cover and chill at least 1 to 2 hours before serving.

CHAMPAGNE AND POMEGRANATE GELATIN RING

Serves 8

2 envelopes gelatin
1 cup hot water
1 cup fresh orange juice
2 cups champagne (2 "splits" of champagne will do, with the addition of extra juice enough to make 2 cups)
1¾ cups drained, brandied dark bing cherries
2 pomegranates
¼ cup chopped walnuts
Garnish of watercress
Mayonnaise

Dissolve envelopes of gelatin in 1 cup hot water. When slightly cooled, add freshly squeezed orange juice. Stir well and pour into glass bowl. Place bowl in a larger one filled with cracked ice and stir liquid until it thickens to a heavy syrup. Add champagne, the dark cherries, the seeds and juice of the pomegranates and ¼ cup of chopped walnuts. Stir gently but constantly until mixture starts to solidify. Place in 6-cup ring mold and refrigerate. When fully set, unmold and serve garnished with watercress and small bowl of mayonnaise placed in center. *This looks lovely on a Thanksgiving buffet table and goes well with roasted turkey or ham.*

CUCUMBER AVOCADO MOUSSE RING

Serves 8 to 10

2 envelopes plain gelatin
½ cup cold water
3 large cucumbers or 4 small ones
¼ cup vinegar
2 teaspoons sugar
½ teaspoon salt
¼ teaspoon white pepper
1 vegetable bouillon cube
3 large avocados, mashed
1 medium onion, grated
½ cup sour cream
½ cup mayonnaise
Green food coloring (optional)

Combine gelatin and water and set aside. Peel cucumbers. Split in half and remove seeds and grate. Measure grated cucumber to make 1 cup. Add vinegar, sugar, salt and pepper and bring to a boil. Remove from heat and add vegetable bouillon cube and softened gelatin. Stir until dissolved. Cool mixture slightly and add mashed avocado, onion, sour cream and mayonnaise. Add a few drops of green food coloring to tint a pale green. Taste for seasoning. Pour into a lightly oiled 2-quart ring mold and chill until set, 4 hours. Turn onto a serving platter and fill center with watercress or marinated shrimp.

CAULIFLOWER VINAIGRETTE

Serves 6 to 8

Cauliflower
Vinaigrette dressing
Anchovies
Black olives
Capers

Soak a trimmed whole head of cauliflower in cold water for 10 minutes. Drain, place in steamer and steam until done, 10 to 15 minutes. Do not overcook; cauliflower should be crisp. Refresh under cold water. Drain; pat dry with paper towels. Cover with vinaigrette dressing and chill. Garnish with rolled anchovies, black olives and dot with capers.

CUCUMBERS FILLED WITH GREEN BEANS AND PEAS

Serves 4

2 medium size cucumbers
½ cup cooked green beans, diced
½ cup cooked peas
Green mayonnaise
Chives

Cut unpeeled cucumbers in half lengthwise. Simmer for 2 minutes (must be firm). Freshen under cool water and dry. Hollow out the seeds and some of the pulp and fill with diced green beans and peas that have been cooked. Chill and cover with green mayonnaise and sprinkle with chives.

Green mayonnaise
2 tablespoons watercress
2 teaspoons chopped fresh tarragon
2 tablespoons spinach
2 tablespoons parsley
1 cup homemade mayonnaise

Boil watercress, tarragon, spinach and parsley for 2 minutes. Drain and rub through a sieve (or put in blender) and add to 1 cup of homemade mayonnaise (see page 143).

SENSUOUS CELERIAC

Serves 4 to 6

1 large celeriac (celery root), about ¾ pound
⅓ cup lemon juice, fresh or bottled
¼ cup mayonnaise
¼ teaspoon Dijon mustard
Salt
Freshly ground white pepper

Peel celeriac and cut into pieces to fit into food processor, using one of the shredder blades so they come out looking like matchsticks, and immediately place in a bowl containing ⅓ cup lemon juice. Shake the bowl to film all matchsticks evenly to keep their creamy color. Drain the celeriac of lemon juice 1 hour before serving and add the mayonnaise, mustard, salt and white pepper. cover and chill. Serve on chilled plates with a garnish of parsley sprigs and a dash of paprika. *The celeriac in mayonnaise will keep for a day in the refrigerator but begins to separate if left longer.*

CHUTNEY CHICKEN SALAD

Serves 6

2 cups diced cooked chicken
1 cup diced canned pineapple
1 cup diced celery
¼ cup chopped peanuts
⅔ cup mayonnaise
2 tablespoons chopped chutney
½ teaspoon grated lime rind
2 tablespoons lime juice
½ teaspoon curry powder
¼ teaspoon salt

Combine all ingredients and chill. Serve in cups of lettuce and garnish with watercress.

DELUXE CHICKEN SALAD

Serves 10 to 12

4 large chicken breasts, split
1 tablespoon butter
1 medium onion, minced
2 teaspoons curry powder
5 ounces chicken stock
1 tablespoon tomato purée
3 tablespoons mango chutney
2 tablespoons apricot jam
2 teaspoons lemon juice
Salt and pepper to taste
8 to 10 tablespoons mayonnaise
8 to 10 tablespoons light cream

Simmer or steam chicken breasts 20 minutes or until tender. Sauté minced onion in butter until soft and about to turn color. Stir in curry powder and cook 1 to 2 minutes. Pour in chicken stock and mix well. Add tomato purée, apricot jam and chutney and simmer over moderate heat until thick. Add lemon juice, salt and pepper. Strain and put in refrigerator to cool slightly. Remove skin and bones from chicken. Chop chicken into bite-sized pieces. Put cooled sauce in a large bowl and gradually whisk in mayonnaise and cream. Add the chicken and mix well. Can be served with rice. Best done a day ahead.

LEAF LETTUCE SALAD

Serves 6 to 8

1 large head leaf lettuce, torn into pieces
1 small onion (preferably red onion), thinly sliced
¾ to 1 cup mayonnaise, as desired
2 teaspoons white sugar
½ pound baby Swiss cheese, shredded
½ box frozen peas

Layer ½ of the ingredients, in order as listed, then repeat. Cover and allow to marinate at least 3 hours, up to 8 hours. Toss well prior to serving. Easy and delicious.

MANGO SALAD WITH TANGY APRICOT DRESSING

Serves 16

2½ cups sliced mangos
3 (3 ounce) packages lemon flavored gelatin
Water
1 (8 ounce) package cream cheese

Drain liquid from the mangos (reserving fruit for later); add enough water to mango liquid to make 4 cups. Then heat liquid to boiling and pour over lemon gelatin to dissolve. Refrigerate the gelatin until slightly jelled. Place mangos and the cream cheese in blender and liquify. Add mango/cream cheese mixture to partially jelled gelatin and blend thoroughly. Pour into individual molds or an 11x7x1¾-inch pan and refrigerate for 6 hours or overnight.

Dressing

1 cup mayonnaise
1 cup sour cream
1 cup apricot preserves

Combine mayonnaise, sour cream and apricot preserves. Unmold the salad onto individual plates or onto a large serving platter. Cover with the dressing.

SALADE NICOISE

Serves 8

2 (2 ounce) tins round anchovy filets
3 (7 ounce) tins white tuna, shredded
1 package frozen Blue Lake variety string beans, cooked
3 ripe tomatoes, peeled and quartered
3 hard-boiled eggs, quartered
Handful black Greek olives
1 small bottle capers
7 to 8 small red new potatoes, boiled (hard not mushy), cubed
Salad greens, washed and chilled
2 small scallions, minced
1 cup chopped celery
½ cup chopped green peppers

Chill everything before mixing. Combine tuna, anchovies, onions, celery, peppers, string beans, olives and capers. Place on salad greens. Garnish with tomatoes, potatoes and egg quarters. Pour over dressing.

Dressing
Several tablespoons mayonnaise
½ cup French dressing

SALADE DU PECHEUR

Serves 5 to 8

18 small scallops
2 large glasses white wine
18 medium shrimp, peeled
1 small (1½ pound) lobster (optional) cooked
Several thin slices smoked salmon
6 fresh white mushrooms, sliced
½ pound sugar peas or French beans, blanched
Juice of 1 lemon
1 bunch watercress

Poach the scallops in white wine for 3 to 5 minutes at simmer. Poach the shrimp in salted water for 3 minutes. Decorate a large platter as follows: distribute watercress on platter; then arrange peas or beans and mushrooms around edge of platter; display scallops, shrimps and lobster in lines on top of watercress; garnish with salmon thongs.
Refrigerate and pour dressing just before serving.

Dressing
4 tablespoons olive oil
Juice 1 lemon
Salt
White pepper

RICE AND ARTICHOKE SALAD

Serves 6 to 8

1 package chicken-flavored rice and vermicelli mixture
4 scallions, sliced
½ green pepper, chopped
12 medium stuffed green olives
2 (6 ounce) jars marinated artichoke hearts
1½ teaspoons curry powder
⅓ cup mayonnaise

Cook rice mixture according to package directions. Do not overcook. Rice should not be soft. Cool. Combine in a serving dish with onions, pepper and olives. Drain artichoke hearts and reserve marinade. Cut the artichoke hearts into small pieces. Add marinade and curry powder to mayonnaise. Pour over rice and stir gently. Serve chilled.

SHRIMP SALAD AND HOMEMADE MAYONNAISE

Serves 8

2 cups cooked and peeled shrimp
2 teaspoons lemon juice
2 to 3 teaspoons minced onion
2 cups diced celery
1½ to 2 cups sliced fresh mushrooms
Salt and paprika to taste

Mix together above ingredients. Chill thoroughly. Just before serving toss with enough homemade mayonnaise to bind. Serve on a bed of lettuce with a side dish of extra mayonnaise.

Dressing
1 egg
1 teaspoon salt
½ teaspoon dry mustard
¼ teaspoon paprika and red pepper
2 tablespoons vinegar or lemon juice
1 cup salad oil

Mix all ingredients except oil in food processor. Add oil in slow stream. Mayonnaise is proper consistency when all the oil is in. Refrigerate until needed.

SHRIMP AND PASTA SHELLS SALAD

Serves 10

4 dozen shrimp, cleaned and cooked
1 pound pasta shells
2 cups cooked fresh peas
2 cups mayonnaise
⅔ cup scallions, finely chopped
3 tablespoons tarragon wine vinegar
⅔ cup herbs, finely chopped (fresh dill, basil, rosemary, etc.)
2 tablespoons capers
Heavy sprinkling of freshly ground pepper
Salt, if desired
Garnish: Chopped parsley or hard-boiled egg or both

Cut the cooked shrimp in half. Cook the pasta *al dente* in 6 quarts of boiling salted water for about 13 minutes or until just tender. Cool. Combine the pasta, shrimp, peas and all the remaining ingredients except for garnish in large, decorative bowl. Add garnish. Serve with a dry white wine or an interesting beer. *If you use frozen peas, just pour boiling water over them in a sieve. Drain well.*

MILLIE'S SHRIMP MOLD

Serves 8 to 10

1 can cream of mushroom soup
2 (3-ounce) packages cream cheese
2 (6½-ounce) cans shrimp
1 tablespoon gelatin (1 package)
2 tablespoons cold water
1 cup mayonnaise
½ cup chopped celery
3 green onions, chopped
Dash lemon juice

Over low heat melt soup and cream cheese. Mash shrimp. Dissolve gelatin in cold water. Add shrimp, then stir in the rest of the ingredients. Pour in a 4-cup mold. Chill for at least 4 hours. Serve with crackers. *This is delicious stuffed in an avocado half and served as a salad.*

GERMAN STYLE SLAW

Serves 6 to 10

1 large head cabbage, shredded
1 medium onion, minced
1 cup sugar
¾ cup salad oil
1 cup vinegar
1 tablespoon salt
1 teaspoon dry mustard

Combine the shredded cabbage and onion in a wooden bowl. Mix the remaining ingredients in a saucepan and bring to a full rolling boil. Pour over the cabbage mixture and mix well. Cover tightly with plastic wrap and chill in the refrigerator.

"Sheffield Plate" four-bottle wine cooler purchased by Washington in 1790.

SPINACH MOUSSE SALAD

Serves 6 to 8

2 (10-ounce) packages frozen chopped spinach
1 (10½-ounce) can consommé
2 envelopes unflavored gelatin
½ teaspoon salt
½ teaspoon celery salt
1 small onion, quartered
Freshly ground black pepper
1 cup sour cream

Pour ½ the consommé over the spinach and cook over medium heat only until the spinach thaws. While spinach is cooking, soak 2 envelopes of unflavored gelatin in remaining consommé. When spinach is cooked, stir gelatin/consommé mixture into it. Mix well. Remove from stove and cool somewhat. Combine remaining ingredients and add this mixture to spinach. Separate into 2 lots and blend each batch thoroughly in electric blender. Pour into a 6 to 8-cup mold coated with oil. Chill until firm. To serve, invert onto a serving platter and garnish with chopped hard-boiled eggs, lettuce and cherry tomatoes. Serve with mayonnaise.

FRESH SPINACH SALAD WITH SWEET SALAD DRESSING

Serves 4 to 6

1 large package fresh spinach
1 can Mandarin oranges, well drained
8 slices crisp bacon, crumbled

Wash the spinach carefully, removing all coarse stems. Dry completely. Combine in a salad bowl with the Mandarin oranges and crumbled bacon and toss with Sweet Salad Dressing which has been mixed and chilled in advance.

Sweet Salad Dressing

¼ cup sugar
1 cup salad oil
½ cup catsup
⅓ cup cider vinegar
2 tablespoons Worcestershire sauce
1 medium onion, grated

Make the dressing a day ahead or quadruple it and keep on hand. Chill 24 hours before serving.

TOMATOES BABACHE

Serves 8

8 ripe tomatoes
1 (14 ounce) can artichoke hearts
1 jar pickled mushrooms

Scoop out tomatoes. Stuff with artichoke hearts and pickled mushrooms. Fill with sauce. Serve on lettuce.

Sauce
1 pint mayonnaise
½ pint sour cream
1 tablespoon curry
Salt
Pepper
Juice of ½ lemon
1 small onion, grated

Mix together mayonnaise, sour cream, curry, pinch of salt, dash of pepper, lemon juice and grated onion.

WILD RICE STUFFED TOMATOES WITH BASIL

Serves 4

4 large ripe tomatoes
1½ cups cooked and cooled wild rice
3 tablespoons chopped fresh basil
3 scallions, finely chopped with some of the green tops
2 teaspoons olive oil
¾ teaspoon garlic salt

Cut a 1-inch slice off the top of each tomato. Scoop out the inside pulp, being careful not to bruise the tomato shell. Chop the tomato pulp and drain excess liquid. Combine pulp with the wild rice, basil, scallions, olive oil and garlic salt. Toss lightly. Fill tomato cases with the rice mixture. Serve on a bed of lettuce leaves. May also be served as a hot vegetable. *One-third cup of uncooked wild rice will equal about 1½ cups of cooked rice.*

FRESH VEGETABLE SALAD

Serves 8

2 cups fresh raw broccoli flowerets, no stems
2 cups fresh raw cauliflower flowerets, no stems
1 cup fresh celery hearts, sliced
1 cup fresh parsley, snipped, no stems
8 ounces fresh mushrooms, sliced
1 tin black olives, pitted and sliced (drained weight 6 ounces)
1 tin water chestnuts, sliced (drained weight 5 ounces)
2 packages Italian salad dressing mix or Monticello French Dressing (page 149)

Wash and drain broccoli and cauliflower. Place all ingredients except broccoli and parsley in a glass container such as a 9x13-inch pyrex dish. Use 1 package dry salad dressing mix sprinkled over the mixture. Use the other package of salad dressing mix; make according to directions on package. Pour over the mixture. Marinate at least 6 hours. Leave broccoli and parsley to be added just before serving. If marinated for a long period in a dressing with vinegar, green vegetables will turn gray.

CURRIED MAYONNAISE FOR COLD LOBSTER

Yield: 1½ cups

1 egg
1 tablespoon lemon juice
1 teaspoon prepared mustard
¼ teaspoon black pepper
1 teaspoon curry powder
1½ cups light salad oil

Put egg, lemon juice and seasonings in a food processor or blender. Blend for a few seconds and with motor still running, pour oil into mixture very slowly. Mayonnaise will keep fresh in a container in the refrigerator for a week or more. Serve with cold boiled lobster.

HOT RUM SAUCE FOR AVOCADOS

Serves 4

2 tablespoons butter
1 tablespoon warm water
1 tablespoon red wine vinegar
1 tablespoon sugar
1 tablespoon Worcestershire sauce
1½ teaspoon catsup
½ teaspoon dry mustard
4 cloves
¼ teaspoon salt
Several dashes hot pepper sauce
1 tablespoon dark rum
2 avocados

Combine all ingredients except rum in saucepan. Bring mixture to boil and stir. Reduce heat to simmer and cover and stir occasionally. Cook for 20 minutes. Remove and discard cloves, add 1 tablespoon dark rum and cook sauce for 2 minutes longer. Halve and seed 2 avocados; score the sides lightly. Divide warm sauce into chilled or room temperature avocados. Recipe can be doubled, reheated over hot water and refrigerated.

HONEY LIME DRESSING

Yield: 1¾ cups

½ cup mayonnaise
¼ cup honey
2 tablespoons lime juice
½ cup heavy cream

Combine mayonnaise, honey and lime juice. Whip ½ cup heavy cream; fold into mixture. Serve with fruit salads.

MONTICELLO FRENCH DRESSING

Yield: 1 cup

2 teaspoons garlic salt or 1 clove garlic, minced, plus 1 teaspoon salt
½ teaspoon white pepper
⅓ cup olive oil
⅓ cup sesame oil
⅓ cup tarragon wine vinegar

Combine all ingredients and shake well before pouring on salad.

ONION SALAD DRESSING

Yield: 1 quart

1 pint chopped onions
2 teaspoons salt
2 teaspoons black pepper
2 teaspoons dry mustard
2 teaspoons paprika
½ cup sugar
¾ cup vinegar
Enough salad oil to fill a quart jar after all other ingredients have been added

Fill 1-quart jar half full of finely chopped onions. Add salt, black pepper, dry mustard and paprika. Let stand 10 minutes, shaking or stirring a few times. Add sugar and vinegar. Finish filling jar with salad oil. Mix thoroughly. Keep refrigerated. Keeps long and well. Improves with time.

VINAIGRETTE DRESSING

Yield: 1 cup

3 teaspoons minced shallots or green onions with tops
¾ teaspoon dry mustard
½ teaspoon salt
3 or 4 grinds of pepper
2 tablespoons wine or white vinegar
2 tablespoons lemon juice
¼ cup olive oil (good quality)
¼ cup peanut or vegetable oil
1 tablespoon fresh herbs (parsley, tarragon, chervil or basil)

Put all ingredients in screw-top jar and shake vigorously.

Breads

Brick beehive oven in the Family Kitchen. The long-handled iron shovel was used to remove ashes from the fire before placing the bread in the hot oven to bake.

BEER BREAD

Yield: 1 loaf

3 cups self-rising flour
3 tablespoons sugar
1 can beer, room temperature

Preheat oven to 350 degrees. Mix all ingredients together. The dough will be very sticky and lumpy. Spread out on greased cookie sheet (like French bread loaf) and sprinkle a little salt all over the top. Bake for 1 hour or until lightly golden brown. Can be frozen and reheated.

BUTTERMILK HONEY BREAD

Yield: 3 loaves

2 packages yeast
½ cup warm water (115 degrees)
2 cups warm buttermilk
½ cup melted butter
2 tablespoons honey
2 teaspoons salt
1 cup whole wheat flour
7 to 8 cups unbleached white flour

Preheat oven to 375 degrees. Sprinkle yeast over water and stir until dissolved. Combine yeast mixture with the buttermilk, butter, honey and salt. Stir in the whole wheat flour. Gradually stir in enough flour until you have a soft resilient dough. You can do this by hand or with a mixer that has a dough hook. Knead for 10 minutes. Place dough in a warm ceramic bowl that has been buttered, turning the dough to coat with butter. Cover with plastic wrap and a towel. Allow to rise until doubled, about 1 hour. Punch down and allow to rise a second time. Remove from bowl, knead for 1 minute and let rest, covered with a towel, for 10 minutes. Divide into 3 portions, shape into loaves and place in 8½x4½x2½-inch loaf pans. Cover with a towel and allow to rise until dough is about 1 inch above pans, 45 minutes. Bake 30 to 40 minutes. Remove from pans onto a wire rack and brush with butter.

DATE NUT BREAD

Yield: 4 loaves

1½ pounds dates, chopped fine
3 cups boiling water
2 tablespoons salad oil
2 teaspoons salt
1 cup chopped walnuts
1 pound brown sugar
2 eggs
4 teaspoons baking soda
2 teaspoons baking powder
2 tablespoons vanilla
5 cups sifted flour

Preheat oven to 325 degrees. Cover the dates with the boiling water and let stand until cool. To this date and water mixture add all remaining ingredients and mix thoroughly. Pour into non-stick loaf pans or spray regular pans with a vegetable spray. When pouring bread mixture into pans, fill only ½ to ¾ full to prevent the bread from going over the sides. Bake for 1 hour. Bread will be lightly brown and cracked-looking on top. *These loaves make lovely presents. They also freeze well.*

MONKEY BREAD

Yield: 2 rings

¾ ounce yeast or 1 package dry yeast
1 to 1¼ cups milk
3 eggs
3 tablespoons sugar
1 teaspoon salt
3½ cups flour
6 ounces butter, room temperature
½ pound melted butter
Two 9-inch ring molds

In bowl, mix yeast with part of milk until dissolved. Add 2 eggs; beat. Mix in dry ingredients. Add remaining milk a little at a time, mixing thoroughly. Cut in butter until blended. Knead dough; let rise 1 to 1½ hours until double in size. Knead again; let rise 40 minutes. Roll dough onto floured board; shape into a log. Cut log into 28 pieces of equal size. Shape each piece of dough into ball; roll in melted butter. Use half of the pieces in each of buttered floured molds. Place 7 balls in each mold, leaving space between. Place remaining balls on top, spacing evenly. Let dough rise in mold. Brush tops with remaining egg. Bake in preheated oven at 375 degrees until golden brown, approximately 15 minutes.

PUMPKIN BREAD

Yield: 1 large loaf or 6 small loaves

1⅔ cups sifted regular flour
¼ teaspoon baking powder
1 teaspoon baking soda
¾ teaspoon salt
½ teaspoon cinnamon
½ teaspoon nutmeg
⅓ cup shortening
1⅓ cups sugar
½ teaspoon vanilla
2 eggs
1 cup canned mashed pumpkin
⅓ cup water
½ cup chopped walnuts or pecans

Preheat oven to 350 degrees. Grease loaf pan (9x5x3 inches) or 6 small loaf pans. Sift together flour, baking powder, baking soda, salt, cinnamon and nutmeg. Cream shortening, sugar and vanilla. Add eggs, 1 at a time, beating thoroughly after each addition. Stir in mashed pumpkin. Stir in dry ingredients in 4 additions, alternately with water, until just smooth. Do not overbeat. Fold in nuts. Turn batter into prepared pan. Bake until cake tester comes out clean, 45 to 55 minutes. Turn out on wire rack, right side up; cool. Will keep for several days if wrapped in foil in refrigerator or indefinitely in freezer. Bring to room temperature before serving.

QUICK PEASANT BREAD

Yield: Two 7-inch loaves

4 cups whole wheat flour
2 cups unbleached flour
⅔ cup rolled oats (either quick or old-fashioned variety)
1 tablespoon baking soda
1½ teaspoons salt
3 cups buttermilk or sour milk (Note: To sour sweet milk, combine 1 tablespoon white vinegar with enough milk to make one cup.)

Preheat oven to 375 degrees. Blend flours, oats, salt and baking soda. Add milk, stir and then knead lightly. Shape into 2 small balls. Put on oiled and floured baking sheet. Slash a cross on top of each loaf. Bake for 35 to 40 minutes until bread sounds hollow when tapped.

THEODORE'S FAMOUS WHOLE WHEAT BREAD

Yield: 2 loaves

Nourishing whole grain breads formed a very important component of the daily diet of both rich and poor in 18th-century America. Here's how to make a modern adaptation; a bread worthy of being called Food.

2½ cups very warm water
1 envelope dry yeast
1 heaping tablespoon honey
1 tablespoon butter
1 tablespoon salt
¼ cup wheat germ
¼ cup corn meal
¼ cup dry milk or dry buttermilk
3 to 4 cups whole wheat flour
3 to 4 cups white all-purpose or bread flour

Wash off and dry a counter-top area for kneading. With a fork, mix water, honey and yeast in a large glass or ceramic bowl. Add butter and let stand while lining up remaining ingredients.

Stir in salt, wheat germ, corn meal and dry milk. Then start adding whole wheat flour directly from the bag, mixing until the batter is the consistency of pudding. Exact measurement of flour is not important; the volume of water determines the volume of dough. In this receipt, the proportion of whole wheat to white flour is roughly 50/50, and the total volume added may vary with temperature, humidity or brand of flour used. Now add white flour directly from the bag, mixing until batter is dry and hard to stir. Scrape out onto counter, add more white flour and begin to knead. Push hard, using the heels of both palms, turning and folding the dough ball. Add more flour periodically until dough becomes firm, resilient and sweet-smelling; it should no longer stick to your hands and should feel silky and pleasing to the touch. Keep on kneading hard 8 to 10 minutes; you cannot over-knead at this point.

Put dough back in bowl, cover and let rise at room temperature until about doubled in bulk, 45 to 90 minutes. (Timing varies with temperature and humidity also.) Scrape out again and knead lightly about 10 times to break the large bubbles. Do not over-knead at this point.

Grease 2 standard (8x4-inch) loaf pans with butter, not oil. Divide dough and roll gently into loaves. Put into pans, pressing lightly into corners. Allow to rise until tops are above rims of pans, 45 to 90 minutes. Do not jostle pans during final rising. Place very gently in a preheated 375 degree oven and bake 55 minutes. Remove immediately from pans and cool on a wire rack until completely cooled to room temperature. Seal in plastic bags. This bread needs no refrigeration for at least 3 days.

RAISIN NUT BREAD

Yield: 1 large loaf or 2 small loaves

½ cup sugar
1½ cups milk
½ teaspoon salt
1 large egg, beaten
3 cups flour
4 teaspoons baking powder
1 cup chopped nuts
1 cup raisins

Preheat oven to 350 degrees. Put sugar, milk, salt and egg into bowl and stir until sugar dissolves. Sift flour before measuring, then sift twice with baking powder. Add to mixture and stir. Add nuts. Pour into 1 large loaf pan or 2 small pans and let rise for 30 minutes. Bake 40 minutes.

WHITE YEAST BREAD

Yield: 1 loaf

1¼ cups warm water
1 envelope dry yeast
2 tablespoons soft shortening or oil
2 teaspoons salt
2 tablespoons sugar
3 cups flour, unsifted

Preheat oven to 450 degrees. In mixing bowl dissolve yeast in warm water. Add shortening or oil, salt and sugar. Measure flour into cup by spoonfuls to avoid packing down flour. Stir in ½ of amount called for. Keep in mind that brands of flour vary and you might need more or less than the 3 cups. Stir the batter until smooth; add remaining flour and stir. Scrape down sides of bowl. When yeast dough has taken all of the flour it can, cover bowl with cloth and let dough rise until double in size. This will take about 1 hour. Beat dough about 25 strokes. Spread evenly in greased loaf pan, 9x5x3 inches. Cover pan with cloth; allow to rise until about ½ inch from top (about 1 hour longer). Bake for 10 minutes. Lower heat to 325 degrees. Bake 25 minutes longer. Turn bread onto rack.

YELLOW CORN BREAD

Serves 18

1¾ cups corn meal
1¼ cups flour
¼ cup sugar (optional)
2 tablespoons baking powder
¾ teaspoon salt
1½ cups milk
½ cup melted shortening or oil
2 large eggs

Preheat oven to 425 degrees. Combine corn meal, flour, sugar, if desired, baking powder and salt. Add milk and shortening, then beat in eggs 1 at a time. Beat until fairly smooth. Pour into well-greased 9x13-inch baking pan. Bake for 20 to 25 minutes. Cut into 18 pieces, about 2x3 inches each (or bake in 18 muffin cups for 15 to 20 minutes). Serve hot.

EASY SPOON BREAD

Serves 6

1 cup self-rising corn meal
1 teaspoon shortening
1 teaspoon salt
1 cup milk
2 eggs, well beaten

Preheat oven to 350 degrees. Combine first 3 ingredients with 2 cups of water in saucepan. Cook over medium heat until smooth and thick, stirring constantly. Stir in milk. Add eggs and beat well. Pour into greased baking dish. Bake 30 minutes or until set.

SPOON BREAD

Serves 6

1 scant cup corn meal
3 cups sweet milk
3 large eggs, separated
1 level teaspoon salt
3 level teaspoons baking powder
Butter, the size of a walnut

Preheat oven to 350 degrees. Stir corn meal into 2 cups of milk and let mixture come to a boil, making a mush. Remove from heat. Add balance of milk and add beaten egg yolks. Stir in salt, baking powder and melted butter. Fold in stiffly beaten egg whites. Bake in a buttered 2-quart soufflé dish 30 minutes.

OLD VIRGINIA BATTER BREAD

Serves 4

2 cups milk
1 cup corn meal
1 tablespoon butter, soft
3 eggs
1 teaspoon salt

Preheat oven to 350 degrees. Scald milk in small pan and pour slowly over corn meal in large mixing bowl; mix well. Cream butter, eggs and salt until light. Combine with corn meal mixture. Pour mixture into 9-inch greased pan. Bake for 30 minutes or until brown on top.

Tin cannister for storing flour and other dry ingredients.

THE WORSTER HOUSE HOT CROSS BUNS

Yield: 36 buns

2 cups milk, scalded
½ cup sugar
8 tablespoons margarine
1 teaspoon salt
½ cup warm water
2 teaspoons sugar
3 packages dried yeast
2 eggs, slightly beaten
2 teaspoons cinnamon
1 cup raisins
7 or 8 cups flour

Heat 2 cups fresh milk to a scald and remove from the stove. Add sugar, margarine and salt. Stir all these ingredients until well dissolved. In a separate bowl place warm water, sugar and dried yeast and stir well. Set this bowl aside for 4 to 5 minutes. Using a small bowl, mix together eggs, cinnamon and raisins. Add this mixture to your bowl of milk, margarine and salt mixture and blend well. Add the 7 or 8 cups of flour and mix all together. Knead well for at least 5 minutes. Place dough in a well-greased bowl and cover with a damp cloth. Let dough double in size. Punch down and roll the dough out on a well-floured surface. Grease a large cookie sheet well and cut buns out to desired size and place close together on the cookie sheet. Bake in a 400 degree oven for 15 to 20 minutes or until golden brown. Remove from the oven and let a light brushing of melted butter gloss each bun. Mix the frosting for the cross.

Frosting for the Cross

¼ cup butter
¼ cup evaporated milk or heavy cream
Powdered sugar
Vanilla, rum, lemon or orange extract

Melt the butter in a small heavy pan. Remove from the heat and add the milk. Beat in sifted powdered sugar until thick enough to spread. Beat until smooth and add a few drops of flavoring—vanilla, rum, lemon or orange. Using a wide-mouth pastry tube, cross each bun with a wide ribbon of frosting. Serve warm if possible.

HOOSIER BISCUIT

1 teaspoon salt
1 pint milk
6½ cups flour
2 tablespoons brewer's yeast
1 teaspoon saleratus (baking soda)
3 eggs, beaten

Add a teaspoon of salt to a pint of new milk, warm from the cow. Stir in flour until it becomes a stiff batter. Add 2 great spoonfuls of lively brewer's yeast. Put it in a warm place and let it rise just as much as it will. When well raised, stir in a teaspoonful of saleratus dissolved in hot water. Beat up 3 eggs (2 will answer) and stir with the batter. Add flour until it becomes tolerable stiff dough. Knead it thoroughly, set it by the fire until it begins to rise. Roll out, cut to biscuit form, put in pans, cover it over with a thick cloth, set by the fire until it rises again, then bake in a quick oven.

POTATO ROLLS

Yield: 3 dozen rolls

1 cup mashed potatoes
⅔ cup shortening
⅔ cup sugar
1 cup milk, scalded
1 level tablespoon salt
2 eggs
5 cups flour (measured before sifting)
1 cake yeast (dissolved in ½ cup warm water in which the potatoes were originally boiled)

While the potatoes are warm, add the shortening, sugar and salt. To this mixture stir in the eggs, 1 at a time, and then add the dissolved yeast cake. Add the milk (cooled) and then stir in 3 cups of the flour. The other 2 cups can be kneaded in until you have dough of very soft consistency. Let rise until double its bulk and then push down and put in refrigerator, preferably overnight. 1½ to 2½ hours before the meal, make the rolls in tins and let rise over moderate heat. Bake in large muffin tins in moderate oven (325 degrees to 375 degrees) for 15 to 20 minutes.

The Scullery

The kitchen scullery, where dishes were cleaned and prepared for use in the mansion, is one of three rooms on the first floor of the kitchen. According to Martha Washington's will, blue and white china was in "common" or everyday use on the family table. To the right of the fireplace is a small iron stand, where plates were warmed. The staircase leads to servants' quarters on the second floor.

(Photograph by Paul Kennedy)

CORN STICKS

Yield: 14 corn sticks

1 cup flour
¾ cup yellow corn meal
1½ teaspoons baking soda
1½ teaspoons double-acting baking powder
¾ teaspoon salt
1 cup buttermilk
1 cup cooked corn kernels
2 eggs, lightly beaten
3 tablespoons butter, melted and cooled
Two 7-stick corn stick molds, greased with melted lard

Into a bowl sift together the flour, corn meal, baking powder, baking soda and salt. Heat the corn stick molds in preheated 400 degree oven for 10 minutes. Stir the buttermilk, cooked corn, eggs and butter into the flour mixture. Stir the batter until it is just combined. Spoon the batter into the molds, filling each nearly to the top. Bake the corn sticks in the preheated oven for 15 minutes or until they are lightly golden and puffed and transfer them to a serving dish.

BREAKFAST GEMS

Yield: 14 gems

¼ cup grits
½ teaspoon salt
½ cup boiling water
1 cup scalded milk
1 cup corn meal
3 tablespoons sugar
3 tablespoons butter
3 teaspoons baking powder
2 eggs, separated

Preheat oven to 425 degrees. Add grits and salt to boiling water and cook for a few minutes until thick. Add hot milk to corn meal; add sugar and butter. Combine grits, corn meal mixture and baking powder. Cool a bit and add beaten egg yolks and fold in egg whites which have been beaten until stiff. Bake in preheated muffin tins for 15 minutes. *If using self-rising corn meal, leave out salt and baking powder.*

DATE MUFFINS

Yield: About 3 dozen medium-large muffins

1½ cups sugar
½ teaspoon salt
1 cup boiling water
2 large eggs, beaten
2 cups sifted flour
2½ teaspoons soda
½ cup shortening
2 cups KELLOGG'S® BRAN BUDS® cereal
1 cup 100% bran cereal
2 cups buttermilk
1 (10-ounce) package pitted dates

Preheat oven to 375 degrees. Pour boiling water over Bran Buds. Cream sugar and shortening. Add eggs, flour and salt. To Bran Buds and water add 100% Bran and buttermilk. Add dates. Combine all ingredients. Bake for 15 to 20 minutes.

MATTIE'S MUFFINS

Yield: 12 muffins

⅔ cup milk
½ cup corn meal
½ cup flour
½ cup cooked rice
3 teaspoons baking powder
2 tablespoons sugar
½ teaspoon salt
1 large egg
1 tablespoon bacon fat, melted

Preheat oven to 425 degrees. Bring milk to boiling point and add corn meal. Let stand 5 minutes. Add flour, rice, baking powder, sugar and salt. Separate egg yolk from white. Beat egg yolk well and then the egg white until stiff. Stir yolk and bacon fat into mixture. Fold in egg white gently. Pour into preheated muffin tins and bake for 15 minutes.

NANCY'S OATMEAL MUFFINS

Yield: 12 muffins

1 cup oatmeal
1 cup buttermilk
1 large egg
½ cup light brown sugar, firmly packed
½ cup whole wheat flour
½ cup white flour
½ teaspoon salt
½ teaspoon baking soda
1 teaspoon baking powder
½ cup vegetable oil

Preheat oven to 400 degrees. Soak oatmeal in buttermilk 1 hour. Add egg and sugar, beating well. Sift flours with salt, baking soda and baking powder. Fold in the batter with the oil. Pour into greased muffin tin and bake for 15 to 20 minutes.

TEA MUFFINS

Yield: 12 muffins

1 cup flour
1 heaping teaspoon baking powder
1 "salt spoon" salt
1 tablespoon butter or shortening
⅛ cup sugar
1 large egg, separated
½ cup milk

Preheat oven to 350 degrees. Mix flour, baking powder and salt and sift. Cream butter and sugar by hand or with an electric beater. Beat the egg yolk; add milk. Add to butter and sugar mixture and beat well. Stir in dry ingredients very briefly. Fold in egg white, beaten stiff. Fill greased muffin tins two-thirds full and bake for 15 to 20 minutes.

APPLE PANCAKES

Yield: 14 to 16 pancakes

1½ cups sifted flour
1¼ teaspoons baking powder
¾ teaspoon salt
½ teaspoon cinnamon
¼ cup sugar
1 large egg, well beaten
1 cup milk
¼ cup melted butter or margarine
1 cup finely chopped apples

Mix and sift flour, baking powder, salt, cinnamon and sugar. Combine egg, milk, butter and apples. Add gradually to the flour mixture until moistened. Do not over mix. Bake on hot greased griddle. Serve with country sausage and maple syrup.

PETER COOK'S PANCAKE

Serves 2

½ cup flour
½ cup milk
2 large eggs, beaten lightly
Pinch nutmeg
¼ cup butter
2 tablespoons powdered sugar
Juice of 1 lemon

Preheat oven to 425 degrees. Mix flour, milk, eggs and nutmeg together in mixing bowl. Melt butter in shallow 9-inch pyrex baking dish. When butter is very hot and sizzling, pour batter into buttered dish and put immediately in oven. Bake for 15 to 20 minutes until lightly browned and very puffy. Sprinkle with sugar and lemon juice. Serve with your favorite jam. *If double recipe is required, make 2 pancakes in separate baking dishes. Do not combine in one as it will not rise properly.*

NO-BEAT POPOVERS

Yield: 9 to 12 popovers

2 large eggs
1 cup milk
1 cup flour
½ teaspoon salt

Preheat oven to 450 degrees. Break eggs into bowl; add milk, flour and salt. Mix well with spoon (disregard lumps). Fill greased muffin tins three-quarters full. Put in oven. Bake for 30 minutes. Don't peek. *Ingredients must be at room temperature or the popovers won't pop!*

TOASTED MARMALADE TEA SANDWICHES

Yield: 12 to 16 sandwiches

8 slices thin white bread
½ stick butter
Orange marmalade, as needed

Trim crusts from the sliced bread. Melt the butter and, with a pastry brush, coat *both* sides of each slice of bread. Spread 4 buttered slices with marmalade and top with other 4 slices. Toast the sandwiches under the broiler or in a frying pan. Cut into strips or squares. Serve hot.

Desserts & Sauces

"Sheffield Plate" sugar pail, one of a pair ordered by Washington from London in 1784.

ALMOND TORTE

Serves 6

7 eggs, separated
1 cup sugar
4 stale lady fingers
½ pound ground almonds, with skins
1 lemon
2 teaspoons baking powder
½ pint whipping cream

Cream yolks with sugar until very light. Toast lady fingers, crush and add to mixture. Grind almonds and add along with grated lemon peel and juice of same. Fold in well-beaten egg whites, adding baking powder last. Pour mixture into 2 baking tins that have been lightly greased and bake in 350 degree oven for 20 minutes. Whip the cream. When the torte is cold, put together with a filling of ½ the whipped cream and cover the top with the remaining half. *Fresh fruit may be used as a garnish around the cake and/or nuts on the top.*

CHOCOLATE BAVARIAN MERINGUE TORTE

Serves 8 to 10

Whites of 3 eggs
½ teaspoon cream of tartar
¾ cup sugar
¾ cup chopped pecans
3 circles brown paper cut in 8-inch diameter

Beat whites of eggs until frothy. Add cream of tartar and beat until stiff peaks form. Gradually add sugar, 1 teaspoon at a time. Beat until peaks form. Fold in pecans. Spread meringue on brown paper circles thinly; shape into flat shell. Bake at 275 degrees for 45 minutes. Turn off oven. Leave in oven 45 minutes.

Filling
2 cups whipping cream
¾ cup Hershey syrup
1 teaspoon vanilla
Shaved chocolate

Beat cream until stiff. Fold in Hershey syrup and vanilla. Layer meringue, cream, meringue, cream, meringue, cream. Ice outside with cream mixture and top with shaved chocolate. Freeze and thaw slightly before serving.

RED RASPBERRY AND BLACK WALNUT TORTE

Serves 8

6 egg whites
2 cups sugar
1½ teaspoons vinegar or lemon juice
Pinch cream of tartar
1 cup black walnuts, finely chopped
1½ pints red raspberries (reserve 15 or 20 to decorate top)
2 cups whipped cream

Beat egg whites until stiff. Add 1 cup sugar gradually. Add second cup sugar in small amounts, alternating with the vinegar or lemon juice, and the cream of tartar. Beat until the meringue holds stiff peaks. Fold in the finely chopped black walnuts. Butter two 9-inch round cake pans. Line with brown paper. Spread meringue evenly in pans and bake in 300 degree oven for 1 hour or until dry and the color of cream. Cool layers of meringue for 5 minutes. Remove from pans and cool completely. Place 1 meringue layer on serving plate. Spread with ½ the raspberries; then add ½ the whipped cream. Add the second meringue layer. Cover with remainder of raspberries. Swirl the remainder of whipped cream attractively on second layer of raspberries and decorate with the reserved raspberries.

PLAIN PASTRY

Yield: One 2-crust pie or
6 to 7 dozen bite-size shells

1 cup all-purpose flour
⅓ cup vegetable shortening
1 scant teaspoon salt
⅓ cup ice water

Sift flour and salt together, work in the shortening with fingers and when mealy, add the ice water a little at a time. Dough should be soft but not sticky. Handle dough as little as possible. Break off a small portion and roll out thinly, cut and put into pans. Prick the insides with a fork. Bake at 400 degrees for 10 to 15 minutes. Watch carefully! *The shells are good for so many hot things, also various sweet fillings. A dab of real whipped cream and fresh strawberries on top is a beautiful dessert.*

BLENDER PASTRY

Yield: Two 8-inch pie crusts

1⅓ cups all-purpose flour
1 stick (8 ounces) cold butter or 4 ounces butter and 4 ounces lard
1 teaspoon salt (less if you use salted butter)
1 tablespoon sugar (optional)
¼ cup ice water

Use steel blade of food processor. Put into work bowl all ingredients except ice water, first cutting butter into several small pieces. Process until the mixture has the consistency of coarse meal (5 to 10 seconds). With machine running, pour ice water through feed tube in a steady stream. Stop processing as soon as dough forms a ball to insure tender, flaky pastry. May be used instantly or freezes well.

CHOCOLATE BUTTER CREAM PIE— CHOCOLATE WAFER PIE SHELL

Serves 8

Shell
25 or more chocolate wafers
¼ rounded cup sugar
3 to 4 tablespoons soft butter or margarine

Pulverize, between 2 pieces of waxed paper, the chocolate wafers. Add sugar and the butter or margarine that has been allowed to get to room temperature and blend together thoroughly. Press onto the sides and bottom of 10-inch pie plate. Chill for 1 hour, then fill with chocolate butter cream.

Filling
¾ cup butter
1 cup sugar
4 ounces unsweetened chocolate, melted and cooled
2 teaspoons vanilla
4 eggs
2 cups whipping cream

Cream butter with electric mixer. Add and cream thoroughly the sugar, unsweetened chocolate and the vanilla. Add the eggs, 1 at a time, beating well after each addition, until light in color. Whip 1 cup of whipping cream and fold into chocolate mixture. Spoon into chocolate wafer pie shell (10 inches). Chill for an hour or more before serving. Before serving, top pie with remaining cream, whipped. *If chocolate mixture gets dark and runny from overbeating chill and rebeat.*

STRAWBERRY OR BANANA MERINGUE PIE

Serves 6 to 8

5 egg whites
1 cup fine granulated sugar
1 teaspoon vanilla
1 teaspoon vinegar (orange mint is good)
Sliced strawberries, bananas or crushed pineapple
Few drops lemon juice
Whipped cream

The success of the receipt depends upon the proper beating of egg whites and the slow addition of sugar. Beat egg whites with egg beater and when almost stiff start using wire whisk. Add sugar gradually a tablespoon at a time and continue beating until sugar is dissolved. When mixture is stiff, add vanilla and vinegar slowly. Put in 10-inch buttered pie plate and bake at 275 degrees for 1 hour. Make mixture higher around edges so you can fill center with sliced bananas, strawberries or crushed pineapple, which have been sprinkled with a few drops of lemon juice. Cover with whipped cream seasoned with a little vanilla.

PUMPKIN PECAN PIE

Serves 6 to 8

4 eggs, slightly beaten
2 cups canned or mashed cooked pumpkin
1 cup sugar
½ cup dark corn syrup
1 teaspoon vanilla
½ teaspoon cinnamon
¼ teaspoon salt
1 unbaked 9-inch pie shell
1 cup chopped pecans

Combine ingredients except pecans. Pour into pie shell; top with pecans. Bake at 350 degrees for 40 minutes or until set.

LEMON CHESS PIE

Serves 6 to 8

8-inch pie shell

Pre-bake pie shell in 425 degree oven for 7 to 8 minutes. Cool.

Filling

1 cup sugar
4 tablespoons butter
4 eggs, separated
Grated rind and juice 1 large or 2 small lemons

Cream sugar with butter until light. Beat in the egg yolks, 1 at a time. Add grated lemon rind and juice; beat in. Beat egg whites stiff; fold in lightly. Pour the filling into the pie shell and bake at 350 degrees until set and light golden brown, about 25 to 30 minutes.

NANTUCKET CRANBERRY PIE

Serves 6 to 8

Filling

2 cups raw cranberries
½ cup sugar
½ cup chopped nuts

Grease a 10-inch pie plate. Place cranberries on bottom. Sprinkle ½ cup sugar and nuts over the cranberries. Cover with batter and bake at 325 degrees for 35 to 40 minutes.

Batter

2 eggs, beaten
1 teaspoon melted butter
¾ cup melted mayonnaise
1 cup flour
1 cup sugar

For batter, mix sugar and butter and add rest of ingredients.

PEACH PIE

Serves 6

Crust

3 tablespoons butter
¾ cup fine graham cracker crumbs
¼ cup chopped walnuts

To make the crust, melt 3 tablespoons butter over low heat. Off heat, stir in ¾ cup fine graham cracker crumbs and ¼ cup chopped walnuts. Press over bottom and sides of 8-inch pie plate. Bake at 375 degrees until lightly browned, about 8 minutes. Cool completely.

Filling

⅓ cup sugar
2 tablespoons cornstarch
1 cup milk
1 cup sour cream
1½ teaspoons vanilla
1 cup diced ripe, but firm, peeled peaches

Garnish

A few peach slices dipped in lemon juice

Stir sugar and cornstarch together in a 1½-quart saucepan. Gradually add milk, keeping smooth. Stirring constantly over medium heat, cook until thickened and boiling. Boil 1 minute. Remove pan from heat and gradually stir in sour cream and vanilla with wire whisk. Fold in diced peaches. Turn into crust and refrigerate until set, several hours or overnight. Garnish with sliced peaches, if desired.

CHARLOTTE DELIGHT

Serves 8 to 10

2 cups soft bread crumbs
½ cup sugar
⅓ cup butter
3 cups hot stewed apples, sweetened to taste
1 pint fresh raspberries
Whipped cream

Spread crumbs with sugar and butter on jelly roll pan. Bake at 350 degrees, stirring occasionally, until mixture starts to caramelize. Spread a layer of crumbs in glass dish and cover with a layer of stewed apples, then fresh crushed raspberries, then more bread crumbs and repeat. Top with crumbs. Cool and cover with a thick layer of whipped cream. *When fresh raspberries are not available, frozen may be substituted. Drain thoroughly.*

IRISH TRIFLE

Serves 10

1 pound cake
Sweet orange marmalade, strawberry jam, or plum jam
½ cup chopped, toasted almonds
1½ cups sherry

Slice the cake lengthwise, ½ inch thick. Place in cake pan or mold. Spread each slice with marmalade or jam and sprinkle with almonds. Pour over with sherry and allow to stand 12 to 24 hours in the refrigerator.

English Custard
2 cups milk
4 egg yolks
⅛ cup sugar
Pinch salt
Whipped cream

Scald 2 cups milk in the top of a double boiler. Stir in slowly 4 slightly-beaten egg yolks, ⅛ cup sugar and a pinch of salt. Place the mixture over boiling water. Stir constantly until the mixture begins to thicken. Remove from heat to another bowl and stir constantly as it cools. Add before chilling thoroughly 1 teaspoon of dry sherry. Apportion cake on dessert plates and top with custard and whipped cream.

LEMON SPONGE

Serves 15

1½ dozen lady fingers
8 eggs, separated
1½ cups sugar
1½ tablespoons gelatin
Juice and grated rind of 2 lemons
½ cup boiling water
½ cup orange juice
½ pint whipping cream

Beat egg yolks well. Add ½ cup sugar, juice and rind of lemons. Cook in top of double boiler until thick. Soak gelatin in orange juice; add ½ cup boiling water and pour into yolks. Let cool. Beat egg whites and add 1 cup sugar. Fold into yolk mixture. Line spring mold (10 inch) bottom and sides with split lady fingers. Pour in mixture. Refrigerate for at least 8 hours. Release mold and put whipped cream on top.

SOUTHERN ICE BOX CAKE

Serves 10 to 12

3 bars German sweet chocolate
6 eggs, separated
3 tablespoons water
3 tablespoons sugar
1 dozen lady fingers or 1 pound cake
8 ounces whipping cream

Boil water in lower part of double boiler. Melt chocolate, water and sugar in top of double boiler and stir continually. When smooth, take off fire and beat in egg yolks 1 at a time, beating each time. Beat egg whites stiffly and fold into chocolate mixture. Whip cream and set aside. Line a loaf pan or a round mold with waxed paper and put ½ of the lady fingers or thin strips of pound cake in the bottom of the pan. Pour in ½ of the mixture and ¼-inch layer of whipping cream. Put another layer of cake, a layer of chocolate and a layer of cream. Chill at least 24 hours. Cut in slices and serve with whipped cream and garnish with grated chocolate.

CRANBERRY PUDDING

Serves 6 to 8

2 eggs, beaten
2 tablespoons sugar
Pinch salt
½ cup molasses
2 teaspoons baking soda
⅓ cup boiling water
1½ cups sifted flour
1½ cups cranberries, cut in half

Combine eggs, sugar, salt and molasses. In a separate container, put 2 teaspoons of soda in ⅓ cup boiling water. Add to egg mixture. Stir in flour and cranberries. Steam in a buttered rice steamer for 1½ hours. Serve warm with the following sauce.

Sauce
2 sticks butter
2 cups sugar
1 cup half and half

Melt butter. Add sugar and half and half and stir until sugar is dissolved.

JUDGE PETER'S PUDDING

Serves 12 to 16

5½ cups fresh orange juice
½ cup fresh lemon juice
2 cups canned pineapple juice
4 envelopes gelatin
1 cup peeled and seeded grapes
½ cup chopped figs
½ cup chopped dates
½ cup chopped pecans
1 cup fresh orange chunks
½ cup bananas (optional)
2 cups whipping cream
1 tablespoon sugar, or to taste
1 teaspoon vanilla or cognac

Mix fruit juices in large bowl and taste for tartness. Take out 1 cup of juice and soften gelatin in it. Heat another cup of the juice almost to boiling, add to the softened gelatin and stir until dissolved. Add dissolved gelatin to fruit juices and put bowl in refrigerator to chill, stirring occasionally until starting to jell. Meanwhile peel and seed the grapes (it's worth the effort). Chop figs, dates and pecans. Section oranges and cut into small chunks, draining off extra juice. If using bananas, cut them just before folding into the jell. When gelatin is slightly thickened, fold in fruits and nuts, 1 variety at a time, to assure even distribution. Rinse a decorative 8-cup mold with cold water, fill with mixture and chill for several hours or overnight. Unmold onto a pretty plate. Serve with sweetened whipped cream.

THE KING'S PLUM PUDDING

(Receipt used by the Royal Family since the days of George I)

1½ pounds suet, finely shredded
1 pound brown sugar (coarse crystals, Demerara)
1 pound small raisins (sultanas)
1 pound large raisins, stoned and cut in half
4 ounces citron, cut in thin slices
8 eggs (1 pound eggs weighed in their shells)
½ pint milk
4 ounces candied peel, cut in thin slices
1 teaspoon mixed spice
½ grated nutmeg
2 teaspoons salt
1 pound bread crumbs
1 to 2 pounds sifted flour
Wine glass brandy

Beat eggs to a froth and then add to them a half pint of milk and mix the various ingredients. Let mixture stand for 12 hours in a cool place and then put in a mold and steam for 8 hours. This makes 3 ordinary sized puddings. *Among the presents taken to India by Their Majesties George V and Queen Mary were a large number of plum puddings made from this receipt. Serve with hard sauce.*

LEMON SPONGE PUDDING

Serves 6

4 tablespoons unsalted butter
¾ cup sugar
3 large eggs, separated
⅓ cup lemon juice
⅓ cup flour
1 tablespoon grated lemon rind (1 to 1½ large lemons)
1½ cups milk
Pinch cream of tartar
¼ teaspoon salt
Powdered sugar

In large mixing bowl cream together the butter, sugar and egg yolks, 1 at a time, beating well after each. Then add lemon juice, flour, rind and salt. Add the milk in a stream, beating and combining mixture well. In another bowl, beat whites until stiff peaks form, adding cream of tartar as you beat. Stir ¼ of the egg whites into the lemon mixture. Fold in remaining whites gently and thoroughly. Transfer into a 1½-quart soufflé dish, which is lightly greased. Set dish in a deep pan, add boiling water ½ way up sides of dish. Bake in preheated 350 degree oven for approximately 50 minutes, or until puffed and golden brown on top. Sift on powdered sugar. Serve warm or chilled. *The sponge will separate, forming a custard-like sauce on the bottom.*

PERSIMMON PUDDING

Serves 6

½ cup melted butter
1 cup sugar
1 cup flour, sifted
¼ teaspoon salt
1 teaspoon ground cinnamon
¼ teaspoon nutmeg
1 cup persimmon pulp (3 to 4 very ripe)
2 teaspoons baking soda
2 teaspoons warm water
3 tablespoons brandy
1 teaspoon vanilla
2 eggs, slightly beaten
1 cup seedless raisins
Chopped nuts (optional)

Stir together melted butter and sugar. Resift flour with salt, cinnamon and nutmeg and add to butter and sugar mixture. Add persimmon pulp, soda dissolved in warm water, brandy and vanilla. Add eggs, mixing thoroughly, but lightly. Add raisins and nuts, stirring until mixed. Put in buttered steam-type covered mold and steam 2½ hours. Flame at table with brandy.

SAILOR DUFF—A STEAMED PUDDING

Serves 6

1 egg, beaten
2 tablespoons sugar
3 tablespoons melted butter
½ cup dark molasses
½ cup hot water
1 teaspoon baking soda
1 cup white flour

Mix all together and put in a buttered mold with a cover, such as a melon mold. If your mold does not have a lid, heavy-duty foil can be used. Put the mold on a rack in a deep pot. Pour in boiling water to come up halfway. Cover the pot and steam for 1 hour. Turn out pudding and serve with sauce.

Sauce
2 eggs
2 tablespoons sugar
1 cup whipped cream
1 teaspoon vanilla

Beat the eggs with the sugar. Mix into the whipped cream and add 1 teaspoon vanilla.

UNCLE JAMES LIKES IT COLD

Serves 6

2 cups milk
⅓ cup sugar
1 tablespoon butter
2 egg yolks, beaten
⅛ teaspoon salt
1 teaspoon vanilla
1 tablespoon brandy
¼ cup dried currants
½ cup bread crumbs

Scald milk and add the sugar and butter. Pour over beaten egg yolks. Add salt, vanilla, brandy and currants. Mix well and pour into buttered individual casseroles. Add bread crumbs to each one. Set in pan of hot water and bake at 325 degrees for 12 minutes or until just barely firm. Delicious hot or cold.

THE WORSTER HOUSE BAKED INDIAN PUDDING

From their 175 year old receipt

Serves 12 to 16

1 quart milk, scalded
¾ cup corn meal
1 cup molasses (4 glups from a jug)
1 cup brown sugar
2 cups raisins
½ cup REAL butter
2 teaspoons PURE vanilla
1 teaspoon salt
1 teaspoon cinnamon
4 eggs
2 cans evaporated milk (13-ounce size) or 26 ounces heavy cream

Place milk in a double boiler and when the milk is hot, sprinkle the corn meal into the scalded milk. Whip to blend and cook for 10 minutes, stirring every few minutes to keep the mixture smooth. Place in a deep baking pan (8x14x6) the following ingredients, stirring in each as you add them to the baking pan: 1 cup molasses, 1 cup brown sugar, 2 cups raisins, ½ cup butter, 2 teaspoons vanilla, 1 teaspoon salt, 1 teaspoon cinnamon, 4 eggs, 2 cans of evaporated milk or 26 ounces heavy cream. Blend well and add the hot corn meal, stirring to blend. Bake in a very slow oven (250 degrees) for 4 hours and be sure to stir thoroughly every 15 to 20 minutes. Serve hot with your best vanilla ice cream.

WINE JELLY

Serves 10 to 12

2 tablespoons gelatin
½ cup cold water
1⅔ cups boiling water
1 cup sugar
1 cup cream sherry
⅔ cup orange juice, strained
3 tablespoons lemon juice, strained

Soak gelatin in cold water. Add the boiling water to dissolve gelatin mixture. Add sugar, cream sherry, orange and lemon juices. Pour into ring mold and chill until firm. Turn out on platter. Fill center with whipped cream and garnish with chocolate leaves (page 204), if you wish, or serve with pitcher of cream. *Remember, the better the grade of sherry used, the tastier the jelly.*

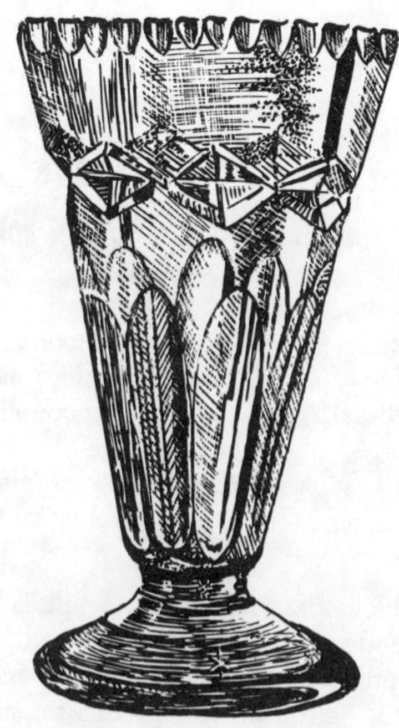

Cut glass jelly glass. "Jelly" was a gelatin dessert.

CRÈME BRULÉE

Serves 6-8

1 pint heavy cream
7 egg yolks
½ cup brown sugar
¼ teaspoon salt
1 teaspoon vanilla

Scald cream in top of double boiler. Beat egg yolks, adding ¼ cup of brown sugar and salt. Add scalded cream slowly to egg mixture. Cook in double boiler, beating constantly, for 6 to 7 minutes or until mixture coats spoon. Remove from heat and add vanilla. Pour into a baking dish. Cover and refrigerate. About an hour before serving, cover top of mixture with remaining brown sugar. (Depending on size of dish you may need a little more.) Glaze under broiler. Return to refrigerator until time to serve.

OLD FASHIONED FLOATING ISLAND

Serves 4

1 pint milk
4 eggs, separated
1 teaspoon vanilla
Sugar to taste

Heat milk in double boiler. Beat yolks. Pour milk over yolks and mix and turn back into boiler. Cook mixture until it thickens to the consistency of soup. Add vanilla. Whip egg whites until stiff. Add sugar to taste. Chill. Serve in bowl with egg white floating on top.

"...I was a good deal surprised to be told...that the Bacon was all of it spoiled in the smoke house...–this fine wet summer...there must be a great quantity of Butter made–which might be sold to bye such necessaries as one wanted about the House..."

Martha Washington to her niece,
Fanny Bassett Washington,
August 4, 1793.

PEACH BRULÉE

Serves 6 to 8

8 to 10 fresh peaches, sliced and peeled
2 tablespoons lemon juice
2 tablespoons white sugar
½ cup sour cream
½ cup light brown sugar

Put the peaches in a 1-quart buttered casserole and sprinkle with lemon juice and white sugar. Spread sour cream on evenly and dot evenly with brown sugar. Put under the broiler just long enough to caramelize. Watch carefully.

SYLLABUB

Serves 8

1 pint whipping cream
½ cup sugar
½ pint half and half
½ teaspoon vanilla
½ cup scuppernong wine
Nutmeg

Chill the liquids, combine all ingredients in a mixing bowl and stir until sugar dissolves; then begin to churn. As the froth rises, lift it off with a large spoon and place it in a serving bowl, repeating this process until the bowl is filled with froth; or the froth may be spooned directly into large wine glasses for individual servings. Sprinkle freshly-grated nutmeg over the syllabub. The froth will hold for 2 hours, chilled. Although the frothiness subsides a bit with time, the dessert is delicious the following day. *This version of syllabub is a light and elegant dessert made distinctive by the use of scuppernong wine for flavor and a syllabub churn for frothiness. Both wine and churn are available commercially now.*

MAPLE CUP CUSTARD

Serves 10

1 quart milk
6 eggs
¾ cup sugar
Dash salt
1 teaspoon vanilla
Maple syrup

Put a teaspoon of maple syrup in the bottom of ten ½-cup size custard cups. Beat together the other ingredients and pour on top of the syrup. Set the custard cups in a pan of water and bake at 300 degrees for 1 hour or until custard is firm. Chill and serve.

ENGLISH WINTER FRUIT COMPOTE WITH CUSTARD SAUCE

Serves 8 to 12

Compote

½ cup dark brown sugar
1 cup water
1 cup large pitted, dried prunes
1 cup dried apricot halves
1 teaspoon grated ginger (optional)
1 cup green seedless grapes
2 large oranges, sectioned
1 large can pears
1 large can peaches
2 bananas, sliced
1 cup chopped walnuts
2 tablespoons sherry (optional)

Bring 1 cup water and ½ cup brown sugar to a simmer. Add dried prunes and apricots. Remove from heat, cover and allow to soak for a few hours or overnight. Cut all fruits into bite-size pieces and toss all the remaining ingredients together gently. Chill until serving time. Serve in a crystal or clear glass bowl. Ladle custard sauce over individual servings.

English Custard Sauce

6 tablespoons sugar
1 tablespoon cornstarch
1 pint milk
2 tablespoons butter or margarine
6 egg yolks
1½ teaspoons vanilla
½ cup heavy cream

In medium saucepan combine sugar and cornstarch. Gradually add milk, stirring until smooth. Add butter and cook over medium heat, stirring constantly until mixture thickens and comes to a boil. Boil 1 minute. Remove from heat. In medium bowl slightly beat yolks. Gradually add a little hot mixture and blend well. Stir into rest of hot milk mixture. Cook over medium heat, stirring constantly, just until mixture boils. Remove from heat; stir in vanilla. Strain custard immediately into bowl. Place sheet of waxed paper directly on surface so skin won't form. Refrigerate until cool. Stir in heavy cream. Return to refrigerator until well chilled.

We viewed the gardens and walks, which are very elegant, abounding with many curiosities, Fig trees, raisins, limes, oranges, etc., large English mulberries, artichokes, etc.

Amariah Frost's Diary, 1797

CANTALOUPE A LA MODE WITH WINE-BLUEBERRY SAUCE

Serves 6 to 8

Sauce (1¾ cups)

½ cup sugar
1 tablespoon cornstarch
3 thin lemon slices
¾ cup port wine
2 cups blueberries (fresh or frozen)

Vanilla ice cream
Cantaloupe, peeled and sliced into rings

In a small saucepan combine sugar, cornstarch, lemon slices and wine. Simmer about 5 minutes or until clear. Remove from heat. Remove lemon, add blueberries and chill thoroughly. Spoon ice cream into melon rings and top with the chilled blueberries.

APPLE CRISP

Serves 4 to 6

¼ cup flour
1 cup brown sugar
½ cup butter, softened
1 cup slightly crushed corn flakes
2 pounds apples (Granny Smith, if possible), peeled and sliced
1 tablespoon lemon juice
Warm cream
½ cup chopped walnuts

Preheat oven to 375 degrees. In a bowl mix flour, brown sugar and butter and blend with fingers. Add corn flakes. Arrange apples in a buttered baking dish and sprinkle with lemon juice and top with corn flake mixture. Bake for 30 minutes and serve with warm cream and top with walnuts.

APPLE DUMPLINGS

Serves 6

Pastry

2½ cups flour
3½ teaspoons baking powder
¾ teaspoon salt
½ cup shortening, cold
¾ cup milk

Sift flour, baking powder and salt. Cut in shortening until it looks like small peas. Stir in the milk with a fork until mixture forms a ball. Turn out on pastry board or cloth. Fold and turn lightly. Wrap in waxed paper and chill.

Apples

6 medium-sized apples, peeled and cored
¾ cup sugar
Juice of ½ lemon
¼ teaspoon cinnamon
¼ teaspoon nutmeg

Roll chilled pastry in six 4-inch squares. Place an apple on each square. Fill each core with the sugar, lemon, cinnamon and nutmeg mixture. Fold over the points of the pastry and pinch corners together on top. Arrange in a large shallow pan.

Syrup

2 cups sugar
2 cups water
Juice of 1 lemon
3 tablespoons butter or margarine

Boil sugar, water, lemon juice and butter until it forms a thin syrup. Pour syrup over the pastry-wrapped apples and bake in a hot oven (425 degrees) for 10 minutes. Reduce the heat to moderate (350 degrees) and bake 35 minutes. Serve hot. Can be served with cream.

PEARS WITH MINCEMEAT

Serves 6

3 ripe Anjou pears
3 tablespoons butter
1 cup mincemeat
1½ tablespoons lemon juice
2 tablespoons brandy
¼ cup water
Sour cream

Wash 3 pears, cut in half lengthwise and core. Mix mincemeat, lemon juice and brandy. Butter a 9-inch pie plate. Put water in bottom of plate. Put 3 tablespoons of the mincemeat mixture into each pear. Bake at 350 degrees for 30 minutes. Serve with sour cream passed separately.

POACHED PEARS WITH RASPBERRY SAUCE

(Elberta peaches may be used just as well)

Serves 6

6 pears, slightly ripened
4 cups water
2 cups sugar
1 tablespoon fresh lemon juice
1 teaspoon grated lemon rind
1 cinnamon stick
3 whole cloves
Inch or 2 of vanilla bean, or use 1 tablespoon vanilla

Peel the pears and drop in a bowl of water with a little lemon juice in it to keep the pears from discoloring. Bring above ingredients to a full rolling boil in a saucepan with very high sides. Add the pears and then cover and keep boiling until the pears are tender when stuck with a fork. This will probably take 30 minutes. When done they should be translucent. Cool in the juice, cover and refrigerate. They are better if they sit overnight. Serve masked in raspberry sauce. A fancy touch is to make chocolate leaves to place beside them on the plate (see page 204).

Raspberry Sauce

1 (10 ounce) package frozen raspberries
1 tablespoon fine sugar
1 tablespoon kirsch (optional)

Thaw frozen raspberries and put through a blender or food processor. Whir until thickened. Strain through a sieve into a bowl and add sugar and kirsch, if desired. Cover tightly and refrigerate.

GLAZED ORANGES WITH GINGER AND ALMONDS

Serves 8

8 large navel oranges
4-inch piece fresh ginger
3 cups sugar
1½ cups water
2 tablespoons orange liqueur (or more to taste)
1 small package slivered almonds, lightly browned in 2 tablespoons butter in 250 degree oven

Carefully remove peel from oranges with a vegetable peeler. Be sure to remove *all* the white pith from peel. Cut peel into 2-inch long match stick pieces. Bring 2 quarts of water to boil. Cook peel 7 minutes. Drain and refresh under cold water. Peel and cut ginger into 2-inch long match stick pieces. Bring sugar and water to boil, cooking slowly until syrup is clear. Put a lid on pan and cook another 2 minutes. Remove lid and cook syrup to 245 degrees on candy thermometer. Add orange peel and ginger and cook 5 minutes longer, stirring. With a sharp knife, peel all remaining white pith from oranges. Pull white tail from center. Cut a small slice off bottom of each orange so that it will sit straight. Place oranges in flat-bottomed dish with sides. Pour syrup, ginger and orange peel over oranges. Refrigerate. Before serving, sprinkle lightly-browned almonds over oranges.

A Madeira glass owned by Washington.

APRICOT SOUFFLÉ

Serves 4 to 6

6 egg whites
1 pinch salt
1 tablespoon baking powder
1 cup dried cooked apricots that have been run through a sieve or puréed in a food processor
1 cup sugar
½ pint whipped cream

Add salt to egg whites and beat until very dry. Add baking powder and then add sugar slowly, beating constantly. Add slowly, by the spoonful, the sieved apricots. Put in greased baking dish, set in a pan of hot water, and bake in a slow (350 degree) oven for about 40 minutes. Serve at once or soufflé will fall. If desired, serve with whipped cream, *very* lightly sweetened.

COLD CHOCOLATE SOUFFLÉ

Serves 8

1 package gelatin
½ cup cold water
½ cup boiling water
5 eggs, separated
1 cup sugar
1 cup milk
5 squares unsweetened chocolate
1 tablespoon vanilla
1 cup heavy cream
¼ cup powdered sugar
1 tablespoon vanilla
Toasted almonds

Put gelatin in cold water and let rest in cold water until soft. Then dissolve it thoroughly in hot water. Beat the yolks with sugar until light colored and smooth. In a double boiler melt chocolate with milk and add yolks, gelatin and vanilla and remove from the heat. Cool to lukewarm. Beat egg whites until firm. Fold into chocolate mixture and pour into soufflé dish. Refrigerate 8 hours. When ready to serve, whip the cream until stiff. Sweeten with sugar, flavor with vanilla and put on top of the soufflé. Sprinkle with almonds. *The soufflé should not sit for more than 8 hours or it will be too stiff. Do not beat the egg whites too stiffly.*

PUMPKIN SOUFFLÉ

Serves 6 to 8

1½ cups sugar
2 tablespoons all-purpose flour
1 teaspoon cinnamon
½ teaspoon nutmeg
½ teaspoon allspice
½ cup butter or margarine, softened
2 cups pumpkin, cooked and mashed
8 eggs, separated
2 tablespoons powdered sugar
1 cup whipped cream

Combine sugar, flour, cinnamon, nutmeg and allspice in the top of a double boiler. Cream in the butter and add pumpkin, beating well. Add egg yolks, 1 at a time, beating well after each addition. Stir over boiling water for 8 to 10 minutes, permitting the mixture to thicken slightly. Set aside to cool well. Preheat oven to 325 degrees. Beat egg whites until stiff but not dry and fold into the cooled pumpkin mixture. Bake at 325 degrees in a buttered, powdered sugar-dusted 9-inch soufflé dish set in a pan of hot water for 45 to 55 minutes or until done. Serve immediately with whipped cream.

MARMALADE SOUFFLÉ WITH CREAMY CUSTARD SAUCE

Serves 4

5 egg whites, room temperature
½ cup tart orange marmalade
1 tablespoon lemon juice
2 tablespoons granulated sugar

Butter top half of double boiler (2½ pints) including inside of lid. Have water boiling in bottom. Beat egg whites very stiff. Soften marmalade with juice; add sugar. Fold into egg whites. Cook over boiling water; do not let water stop boiling. Turn soufflé out in shallow bowl. Serve immediately with sauce.

Creamy Custard Sauce
3 egg yolks
2 tablespoons sugar
1 cup milk, scalded
2 tablespoons Grand Marnier
¾ cup heavy cream, whipped
Grated rind 1 orange

Whisk yolks and sugar; add hot milk to eggs. Cook until mixture coats spoon. Cool custard (covered) and add liqueur. Mix into whipped cream. Fold in grated orange rind. More liqueur may be added.

RUM SOUFFLÉ

Serves 6

4 eggs, separated
¼ cup sugar
1 teaspoon vanilla
⅛ teaspoon salt
¼ cup rum

Beat yolks of eggs and sugar well. Add vanilla. Whip whites with salt. Fold into yolks lightly. Pour into baking dish or individual ramekins. Bake at 325 degrees for about 25 minutes or until firm. Pour rum over soufflé at table, light and let burn out.

BLENDER CHOCOLATE MOUSSE

Serves 5 to 6

6 ounces semi-sweet chocolate
2 tablespoons coffee liqueur
1 tablespoon orange juice
2 egg yolks
2 whole eggs
1 teaspoon vanilla
¼ cup granulated sugar
1 cup heavy cream

Melt chocolate with coffee liqueur and orange juice over low heat; set aside. Put egg yolks, whole eggs, vanilla and sugar in blender. Blend 2 minutes at medium speed. Add cream and blend 30 seconds. Add chocolate mixture and blend. Pour into containers and refrigerate for 1 hour before serving. This may be served with cream.

...send me 2 or 3 Bush. of Chocolate Shells such as we've frequently drank Chocolate of at Mt. Vernon, as my Wife thinks it agreed with her better than any other breakfast...

Burges Ball to George Washington
February 13, 1794

BLACKBERRY MOUSSE

Serves 4 to 6

1 tablespoon gelatin
¼ cup lime juice
½ cup boiling water
⅓ cup sugar
1 cup blackberries
2 eggs
1 cup heavy cream

Sprinkle gelatin in lime juice. After it has softened, add ½ cup boiling water. Place mixture in blender. Add 2 eggs, ⅓ cup sugar, 1 cup blackberries. Then add at highest speed heavy cream. Butter a mold. Pour mixture in mold. Place in refrigerator for 4 hours. Unmold. Garnish with whole blackberries and whipped cream, if desired.

LEMON ANGEL MOUSSE

Serves 8

2 cups sweetened, condensed milk
1 cup fresh lemon juice
2 egg yolks
2 tablespoons grated lemon rind
2 cups heavy cream, whipped to form peaks

Pour milk into a bowl and stir in lemon juice until well blended and thickened. Add egg yolks and beat well. Add 1 tablespoon lemon rind. Fold mixture into whipped cream and pour in parfait glasses. Top with remaining lemon rind and chill 4 hours.

ORANGE MOUSSE

Serves 6

¾ cup sugar
Grated rind of 1 orange
¼ cup cold water
1 envelope gelatin
2 tablespoons cold water
⅔ cup orange juice
2 tablespoons lemon juice
1½ cups heavy cream, whipped

Put the sugar and grated orange rind and ¼ cup water in a saucepan and boil for 1 minute. Soak the gelatin in the 2 tablespoons of water and then dissolve it in the hot syrup. Add the orange juice and lemon juice. Pour into a mold and place over a bowl of ice to chill until the mixture begins to thicken. Stir frequently. Fold in the whipped cream. Allow at least 4 hours in the refrigerator before serving.

FRUIT SHERBET

Serves 16 to 18

2 cups sugar
3 cups water
2½ cups drained, crushed pineapple
1 (12 ounce) can apricot nectar juice
1 (#2) can pineapple juice
1 (#2) can apricot halves, puréed
Juice of 3 lemons
Juice of 2 limes
1 quart fresh orange juice

Add sugar to water and stir over low heat until completely dissolved. Boil 5 minutes. Chill. Add other ingredients to chilled sugar/water base. Mix well and freeze in ice cream freezer packed with ice and rock salt according to freezer directions. After freezing, put sherbet in mold and place in freezer. When ready to serve, remove from mold and place fresh fruit around the base. Makes about 3 quarts.

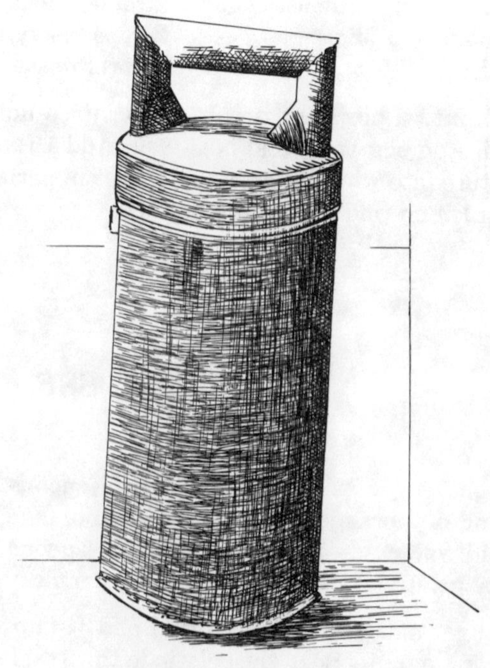

Ice cream freezer.

FRUIT SYRUPS

Yield: 1 pint

1 quart fresh berries
1 cup water
2 cups sugar

Put washed berries in a 2-quart saucepan with 1 cup water and bring to the boiling point. Simmer for 10 minutes. Pour contents of pan into a strainer lined with cheesecloth which has been set on a 1-quart measuring cup. Gently press out as much juice as possible. Discard pulp and measure juice. For each cup of juice add 1 cup of sugar. Return to heat and bring to a boil, stirring to dissolve sugar. Skim off froth as mixture boils for 2 or 3 minutes. Pour into hot, sterilized jars and seal. (Store in refrigerator if not sealed.) Use as sauce for pudding, cakes, mixed fruits or ice cream or as a base for beverages.

MAPLE CREAM SAUCE

Yield: 1 cup

1 cup maple syrup
½ cup whipping cream

Simmer gently 1 cup maple syrup for 30 minutes. In another pan bring ½ cup whipping cream to almost boiling point. Add to syrup and boil together 10 minutes. Take off the stove and when cool whip vigorously. Good warm or cold on ice cream or pudding.

SUPER SAUCE

Yield: 1 cup

1 cup powdered sugar
1 tablespoon butter
1 egg, separated
1 cup cream
Vanilla, rum or brandy

Cream sugar and butter. Add beaten yolk of egg. Stir in well-beaten white of egg. Just before serving add cup of cream, whipped and flavored with vanilla, rum or brandy. Can be used for any cakes or fruits.

DESSERT SAUCE

Serves 4

½ cup sugar
½ cup margarine
2 egg yolks
½ cup fresh lemon juice

Cream sugar and margarine. Add egg yolks. Blend thoroughly. Add fresh lemon juice. Cook in double boiler until thick and glossy. Very good on poundcake. Marvelous on angel or white cake.

BRANDY WHIPPED CREAM SAUCE

Yield: 2 cups

1 egg
⅓ cup melted butter
1 cup sifted powdered sugar
Dash salt
1 tablespoon brandy flavoring
1 cup whipped cream

Beat egg until light and fluffy. Beat in butter, powdered sugar, salt and brandy flavoring. Beat whipping cream until stiff. Gently fold into first mixture. Cover and chill until ready to serve. Stir before spooning on pudding.

Kitchen Interior

He keeps an excellent table and a stranger, let him be of what Country or nation, he will always meet with a hospitable reception at it. (Nicholas Cresswell, 1777). George Washington humorously described his home as a "well-resorted tavern", at which no traveller on the North American continent failed to stop. The kitchen where meals were prepared for his family and guests is now furnished with a number of Washington pieces, including the marble mortar on the stool. The makings of a pie are shown here on a period pastry table. A small oven is recessed in the wall to the right of the fireplace.

(Photograph by Paul Kennedy)

Cakes, Cookies & Candies

A "beeskep" or straw beehive, of a type used in the 18th century. George Washington's fondness for honey is well documented.

FRESH APPLE CAKE—WALTER HEACOCK

Serves 8 to 12

5 small apples, cut in cubes
2 cups sugar
1 cup butter, melted, or 1 cup liquid shortening
3 cups flour
2 teaspoons baking soda
1 teaspoon salt
2 teaspoons cinnamon
1 teaspoon nutmeg
1 teaspoon allspice
2 whole eggs
1 cup raisins
1 cup chopped nuts

Mix apple cubes with sugar and set aside for 10 minutes. Melt butter. Sift together flour, baking soda, salt, cinnamon, nutmeg and allspice. Mix the shortening with 2 eggs; add apple and sugar mixture. Add dry ingredients just to mix. Add raisins and nuts. Bake in greased 13x9-inch pan at 350 degrees for about 50 to 60 minutes. Let cool for 10 minutes. Serve plain or with whipped cream or vanilla ice cream.

APRICOT NECTAR CAKE

1 package Duncan Hines yellow cake mix
4 eggs
¾ cup apricot nectar
¾ cup oil
3 teaspoons almond extract

Mix ingredients and beat for 2 minutes with an electric beater or 300 quick beats by hand. Put ingredients in a well-greased and floured tubular cake pan, 10x4 inches. Bake 45 to 50 minutes in 350 degree oven. Remove from oven and let stand for 10 minutes. While still warm, make holes with ice pick or knitting needle on top and glaze.

Glaze

1½ cups powdered sugar
Juice and rind of 2 lemons

DANISH LOAF CAKES

¾ cup blanched almonds, finely chopped
3 cups all-purpose flour
4 teaspoons baking powder
½ teaspoon salt
2 cups heavy cream
2 teaspoons vanilla
½ teaspoon almond flavoring
2 cups sugar
4 eggs
¼ cup pignolia nuts (pine nuts)

Preheat oven to 350 degrees. Butter heavily 2 loaf pans, each measuring 9x5 inches across the top. Coat the sides and bottom of each pan with finely-chopped almonds. Sift together the flour, baking powder and salt. Set aside. Whip the cream in a large bowl with an electric mixer until it holds its shape. Add the vanilla, almond flavoring and sugar. Beat in the eggs 1 at a time. At the lowest speed, stir in dry ingredients. Pour ¼ of the batter into each pan. Sprinkle each with about 2 tablespoons of pignolias. Cover evenly with remaining batter. Smooth the tops and sprinkle with remaining pignolias. Bake 1 hour or until cakes test done. Remove from oven and brush on glaze. Let the cakes cool in the pans. *One-quarter cup finely-chopped almonds may be used instead of the pignolias.*

Glaze

⅓ cup Kirsch, warmed
⅓ cup sugar

GATEAU DE NANCY

Serves 8

4 ounces Maillard's chocolate or bitter chocolate
1 tablespoon rum or brandy
1 tablespoon black coffee
3 ounces sweet butter (6 tablespoons), room temperature
3 tablespoons sugar, to be used only if using bitter chocolate
3 ounces ground almonds
3 eggs, separated
Whipped cream flavored with sugar and rum or brandy

Grease a 3 to 4-cup ring mold and dust with flour or line a greased 7-inch tart pan with removable bottom with greased waxed paper. Break up the chocolate in small bits; melt over low heat with the liquor and the coffee. When smooth and slightly cool, stir in the butter, sugar, if used, and the ground almonds. Blend until smooth and add the egg yolks, stirring well. Beat the egg whites until stiff but not dry. Fold in the chocolate and egg yolk mixture. Fill the pan. Bake in the middle of a 300 degree oven for 35 to 40 minutes. When set, put on a rack to cool. Turn out very carefully; it is fragile. Decorate with whipped cream, sweetened and flavored to taste. *The receipt can be doubled.*

MELT IN YOUR MOUTH BLUEBERRY CAKE

Serves 8

2 eggs, separated
1 cup sugar
¼ teaspoon salt
8 tablespoons margarine, softened
1 teaspoon vanilla
1½ cups sifted flour
1 teaspoon baking powder
⅓ cup milk
1½ cups fresh blueberries
Sugar to sprinkle on batter

Beat egg whites until stiff, adding about ¼ cup of the sugar called for in the receipt. Set aside. Cream margarine; add salt and vanilla. Add remaining sugar gradually. Add unbeaten egg yolks and beat until mixture is light and creamy. Sift 1¼ cups of flour and baking powder together. Add to creamed mixture alternately with the milk. Fold in beaten egg whites. Fold in fresh blueberries, which have been gently shaken in ¼ cup flour so they won't settle. Turn into greased 8-inch pan. Sprinkle granulated sugar on top. Bake at 350 degrees for 50 to 60 minutes.

BRANDY-JAM LOAF CAKE

Serves 8

¾ cup butter
1½ cups sugar
3 eggs, beaten
1 teaspoon ground cloves
1 teaspoon allspice
1 teaspoon nutmeg
1 teaspoon cinnamon
1 cup sour milk or add 1 teaspoon baking soda to sweet milk
3½ cups flour
1 cup strawberry or peach jam
1 cup raisins
1 cup chopped pecans
1 cup chopped preserved citron
1 cup brandy to pour over

Cream the butter and sugar. Add the eggs beaten well with the spices. Add the sour milk alternately with the flour and when well blended, add the jam, raisins, pecans and citron. Fold in gently. Pour into a greased 10-inch tube pan. Bake in moderate oven (350 degrees) for 50 to 60 minutes or until toothpick tested in center comes out clean. Unmold and while still warm, pour brandy over the top.

GRANNY'S LAZY DAISY CAKE

Serves 9

½ cup milk
1 tablespoon butter
2 eggs
1 cup sugar
1 cup sifted all-purpose flour
1 teaspoon baking powder
Pinch salt
1 teaspoon vanilla

Heat milk and butter but do not boil. Beat eggs in large bowl and add sugar. Stir in dry ingredients after sifting together. Add liquid ingredients and flavoring. The mixture will be thin. Bake in a greased 8½x8½-inch square pan at 375 degrees for 25 minutes.

Topping
⅔ cup brown sugar
⅓ cup melted butter
1 cup coconut
4 tablespoons cream

Stir and spread on baked cake and brown under broiler. *This cake can be doubled and baked in a 9x14-inch pan.*

MOUNT VERNON GINGERBREAD

Yield: 24 squares

½ cup butter
½ cup dark brown sugar
1 cup dark molasses
½ cup warm milk
2 tablespoons ground ginger
1 heaping teaspoon cinnamon
1 heaping teaspoon mace
1 heaping teaspoon nutmeg
¼ cup best brandy
3 eggs
3 cups flour
1 teaspoon cream of tartar
Juice and grated rind of 1 large orange
1 teaspoon baking soda
1 cup seedless raisins (optional)

Cream together butter and brown sugar until light. Add 1 cup of molasses and ½ cup warmed milk. Mix well. Mix separately the spices (ginger, cinnamon, mace and nutmeg) and stir into the batter. Add ¼ cup brandy. In a small bowl beat eggs until light and thick. Sift together flour and cream of tartar. Stir eggs and flour alternately into the batter. Stir in the juice and rind of the orange. Dissolve 1 teaspoon of soda in 1 teaspoon of warm water and add this to the batter. Beat batter until light. Add raisins, if desired, and pour into 2 greased and floured pyrex baking dishes (8½x8½-inch size). Bake at 350 degrees for 40 to 45 minutes. Let cool in pans. Turn out on a rack to cool completely before cutting into squares. *This is a very dark and spicy gingerbread, not sweet. Mrs. Washington served it with a glass of Madeira or rum or a mint julep.*

SPONGE CAKE

Serves 6 to 8

3 eggs
6 tablespoons cold water
1 cup sugar
1 cup cake flour
1 teaspoon baking powder
¼ teaspoon salt
¼ teaspoon lemon extract

Separate egg whites from yolks; set aside whites. Beat yolks until light yellow. Gradually add water, beating constantly. Gradually add the sugar. Fold in the flour that has been sifted with the baking powder and add the flavoring. Beat the egg whites until stiff and fold into the mixture. Pour into greased and floured 10-inch tube pan. Bake at 350 degrees for 45 minutes.

POUND CAKE SOAKED IN ORANGE JUICE

Serves 8

1 cup shortening
2 cups sugar
4 eggs
1¼ cups buttermilk
1 teaspoon baking soda
3 cups flour
½ teaspoon lemon extract
1 tablespoon orange rind
Pinch salt
1 cup orange juice
2 cups sugar

Cream together the shortening and sugar until light and fluffy. Add the eggs one by one, beating hard after each addition. Add the buttermilk mixed with the soda alternately with the flour. Add the lemon extract, orange rind and salt. Grease tube pan and line with waxed paper. Grease the paper. Bake 1 hour at 375 degrees. Remove from oven and lift from the pan. Spoon a mixture of the orange juice and sugar over the hot cake slowly to let it absorb.

...He breakfasts on tea and caks [sic] made from maize;...he makes slices spread with butter and honey...

Julian Niemcewicz's Journal, 1798

RUM CAKE

Serves 15

1 yellow cake mix
1 (3½ ounce) package instant vanilla pudding
1 cup water
½ cup Crisco oil
4 eggs
1 cup chopped pecans
1 cup coconut flakes
¼ pound butter
½ cup dark rum

Mix first 5 ingredients. Fold in nuts and coconut flakes. Pour into tube angel cake pan. Bake for 50 minutes at 350 degrees. Melt the butter with the rum and at this time pour this mixture over the cake and continue to bake for 10 more minutes. Let cake cool for several hours as it is a very rich cake and easily breaks up unless thoroughly cool. Keeps well in the refrigerator.

SHERRY CAKE

Serves 8 to 10

1 package yellow cake mix
1 small package instant vanilla pudding mix
1 teaspoon nutmeg
4 eggs
¾ cup vegetable oil
¾ cup cream sherry
Sifted powdered sugar to cover cake

Combine ingredients and beat with electric mixer for 4 minutes. Pour into well-buttered 10-inch bundt pan and bake at 325 degrees for 45 to 50 minutes, or until cake tests done. Cool in pan 15 minutes, then turn out and sprinkle with sifted powdered sugar.

WASHINGTON CAKE (CURRANT POUND CAKE)

Serves 12 to 16

5 cups sifted all-purpose flour
1½ teaspoons baking powder
1 teaspoon nutmeg
½ teaspoon salt
1½ cups butter or margarine, softened
2¾ cups sugar
6 eggs
1½ teaspoons vanilla extract
1 cup milk
1 (11 ounce) package currants

Preheat oven to 350 degrees. Grease well and flour a 10-inch tube pan. Sift flour with baking powder, nutmeg and salt and set aside. In large bowl, with electric mixer at high speed, beat butter with sugar until light and fluffy, takes about 5 minutes. Add eggs, 1 at a time, beating well after each addition. Add vanilla and continue beating until smooth and fluffy. At low speed beat in flour mixture (in fourths) alternately with milk (in thirds), beginning and ending with flour mixture. Beat only until combined. Stir in currants. Turn batter into prepared pan. Bake 1 hour and 20 minutes or until cake tester inserted in center comes out clean.

Sugar cone from which the needed amount would be "nipped" with scissor-like cutters.

ELEGANT BROWNIES

Yield: 30 brownies

1 cup butter or margarine (butter keeps better)
2 cups sugar
4 eggs, add 1 at a time, beating after each
1 cup all-purpose flour
4 ounces bitter chocolate, melted
1 cup chopped pecans or walnuts
1 teaspoon vanilla

Mix all ingredients in a mixing bowl, using 4 ounces of the melted chocolate, and put in a greased oblong pan 9x14x1½ inches. Bake at 325 degrees. Check at 35 minutes. Cool in pan and add the following topping.

Topping
1 cup powdered sugar
4 tablespoons soft butter
Cream

Stir and work together until the proper consistency to spread. Use a little cream if necessary. Spread on top of cake. Let dry. Then dribble in a criss-cross pattern the ounce of melted chocolate across the whole top. When set, slice the cake into small rectangular pieces.

BUTTERSCOTCH GOODIES

Yield: 48 cookies

4 medium eggs
2 cups firmly-packed brown sugar
1 tablespoon butter
1½ cups sifted all-purpose flour
1½ teaspoons double-acting baking powder
1½ cups black walnuts
1 teaspoon vanilla
Powdered sugar

Beat eggs with beater in top of double boiler until blended. Blend in brown sugar and butter. Place this over rapidly boiling water, stirring constantly, just until hot (about 5 minutes). Remove from heat. Sift together flour and baking powder. Add all at once to cooked mixture. Mix until well blended. Stir in walnuts and vanilla. Turn into well-greased and lightly-floured 13x9-inch pan. Bake at 350 degrees for 25 to 30 minutes. Sprinkle with powdered sugar.

MINIATURE CHEESE CAKES

Yield: 80 cakes

3 (8 ounce) packages cream cheese, softened
5 eggs
1 cup sugar
1½ teaspoons vanilla or amaretto

Beat cheese and add eggs 1 at a time, beating well after each addition. Add sugar and vanilla or amaretto and blend well. Fill very small paper baking cups ¾ full. Bake at 300 degrees for 20 to 25 minutes. The cakes will fall slightly when removed from the oven. Cover each cake with ½ teaspoon of topping and bake 5 minutes longer. Decorate with a bit of candied fruit or ground toffee.

Topping
3 cups sour cream
½ cup sugar
1 teaspoon vanilla

Blend cream, sugar and vanilla.

CHEESE CAKE SQUARES

Yield: 36 squares

1 cup crushed graham crackers (usually 16)
½ cup melted butter
1 cup heavy cream
½ cup lemon juice
1 package softened unflavored gelatin (in ¼ cup cold water), dissolve over hot water
8 ounces cream cheese
1 (14 ounce) can Eagle Brand sweetened condensed milk
1 teaspoon vanilla
Grated rind of 2 lemons

Mix crushed crackers with the melted butter. Press ⅔ cup into the bottom of a 9x13-inch baking pan. Reserve the rest. Mix cream and juice and beat until thick. Beat gelatin into cream cheese and the Eagle Brand milk. Then fold in whipped cream with lemon juice and add the vanilla. Pour into cracker-lined pan and refrigerate overnight. Sprinkle grated lemon rind on top. Cut into 1-inch squares. Coat sides in reserved crumbs, leaving top with just lemon rind.

CASSEROLE COOKIES

Yield: 40 cookies

2 eggs
1 cup sugar
1 cup chopped dates
1 cup shredded coconut
1 cup chopped walnuts
¼ teaspoon vanilla
¼ teaspoon almond extract
½ cup powdered sugar

Beat eggs, add sugar and mix well. Incorporate remaining ingredients except for powdered sugar and mix together. Bake in a buttered 1-quart casserole for 25 to 30 minutes at 350 degrees. Stir mixture occasionally during baking. Let mixture cool to touch. Shape into balls and roll in powdered sugar.

DELIA'S GINGER COOKIES

1 cup sugar
1 cup molasses
1 cup butter or margarine, softened
4 teaspoons ginger
½ teaspoon black pepper
2½ cups flour
1 teaspoon baking soda
1 tablespoon water

Mix the first 5 ingredients together and then add the flour to make a soft dough. You may need to add more flour but never use more than 3 cups. Add the baking soda mixed with the water. Chill dough 1 hour. Measure the dough with a teaspoon and roll into marble-sized pieces. Flatten with your hand. Bake on an ungreased cookie sheet at 375 degrees for 10 minutes. Watch carefully. They burn easily.

CHOCOLATE LEAVES

1 ounce unsweetened chocolate
3 ounces semi-sweet chocolate

If you have tart pans in the shape of a leaf or shell or a madeleine pan in the 2-inch size, line them very smoothly with aluminum foil. If without such pans, pick leaves of suitable size and shape from your yard. Camelia leaves are fine. Cover them with the foil. Melt cocolate over hot water in a small pan. Using the back of a teaspoon, coat the foil-lined molds or leaves with a thin layer of chocolate. Put on a tray in freezer until hard. Then carefully peel away the foil.

CONGO SQUARES

Yield: 48 small squares

⅔ cup vegetable shortening
1 pound package brown sugar
3 eggs
2¾ cups flour
2½ teaspoons baking powder
½ teaspoon salt
1 cup pecans
1 small package chocolate chips
1 teaspoon vanilla

Melt shortening and add sugar. Stir until well mixed and cool. Add eggs 1 at a time. Beat well after each addition. Add dry ingredients, nuts, chocolate bits and vanilla. Pour into greased 10½x15½-inch pan. Bake at 350 degrees for 25 minutes. Let cool a little before cutting.

HOPKINS HOUSE COOKIES

Yield: 3 to 4 dozen cookies

1¾ cups flour
⅔ cup sugar
⅔ cup margarine or butter
1 egg
½ cup molasses
1½ teaspoons baking soda
1¼ cups raisins or currants or both
½ teaspoon ground cinnamon
1½ teaspoons ground ginger
½ teaspoon salt

Melt margarine and add sugar. Combine with all other ingredients and let stand in refrigerator several hours or overnight. Place by teaspoon onto a greased cookie sheet, smooth with a knife dipped in milk, and bake at 350 degrees about 10 to 12 minutes. Remove to rack to cool.

FRENCH LACE COOKIES

Yield: Approximately 5 dozen

½ cup light corn syrup
¼ cup butter
¼ cup shortening
⅔ cup brown sugar, firmly packed
1 cup sifted all-purpose flour
1 cup finely chopped nuts

Combine corn syrup, butter, shortening and brown sugar in a saucepan. Bring to a boil and then remove immediately from the heat. Blend in flour and nuts gradually. Drop by rounded teaspoonful onto a greased baking sheet about 3 inches apart. Bake in a slow oven (325 degrees) for 8 to 10 minutes. Cool 1 minute. Remove carefully with spatula.

OATMEAL COOKIES

Yield: 3 dozen cookies

1 cup butter
1 cup granulated sugar
½ cup brown sugar
1 egg
1½ cups sifted flour
1 teaspoon baking soda
1 teaspoon cinnamon
1½ cups quick-cooking oatmeal
¾ cup chopped walnuts
1 teaspoon vanilla

Cream butter and sugar. Add flour sifted with soda and cinnamon. Add egg. Add oatmeal and chopped walnuts and vanilla. Chill thoroughly. Drop by teaspoonful onto greased cookie sheet. Bake at 350 degrees for 10 minutes.

SESAME WAFERS

Yield: Approximately 3 dozen

1 tablespoon butter, softened
1 cup brown sugar
½ cup toasted sesame seeds
3 tablespoons flour
1 egg, beaten
1 teaspoon vanilla extract
½ teaspoon almond extract
¼ teaspoon salt

Preheat oven to 350 degrees. Cream butter and brown sugar; add sesame seeds. Add flour, beaten egg, vanilla extract and almond extract and salt. Drop by teaspoonful onto well-greased cookie sheet. Bake until firm, 5 to 8 minutes. Remove from pans while still warm.

HARD LIQUOR BALLS

1 box vanilla wafers, crushed
3 tablespoons cocoa
3 tablespoons dark corn syrup
1½ cups chopped pecans
Whiskey or rum
Powdered sugar

Mix first 4 ingredients. Pour liquor over, enough to make a dough. Roll into balls and then roll into powdered sugar.

Washington's large mahogany "spirits" chest.

BROWNIE BALLS—ALMOST A CANDY

1 cup sugar
3 tablespoons butter, softened
2 eggs
2 squares bitter chocolate, melted
3½ tablespoons flour
½ teaspoon salt
1 teaspoon vanilla
1 cup chopped pecans

Preheat oven to 350 degrees. Butter an 8-inch square pan. Cream sugar and butter until light and well blended. Add eggs 1 at a time, beating well after each addition. Mix in melted chocolate. Add flour, salt, vanilla and pecans. Bake for just 25 minutes. Allow to cool to slightly warm. Form in small balls (the size of a quarter) by rolling in the palms of your hands. Drop the balls into a bowl of granulated sugar and coat them well. Cool on racks.

OLD FASHIONED DIVINITY

2½ cups sugar
½ cup white corn syrup
½ cup water
¼ teaspoon salt
2 egg whites
2 teaspoons vanilla extract
Chopped nuts, pecans or walnuts (optional)

Mix sugar, corn syrup and water. Stir occasionally and cook until candy thermometer, which is essential, registers 238 degrees. While waiting, beat egg whites, with salt added, until stiff. When syrup registers 238 degrees, pour gradually only ½ into egg whites, beating constantly with electric beater. Cook remaining syrup mixture until thermometer registers 256 degrees. Then add slowly to candy mixture, beating constantly. Add vanilla and chopped nuts (if desired). Continue to beat, only by hand, until a spoonful of candy holds its shape when dropped on waxed paper. Work fast, spooning candy mounds 1 by 1 onto paper. This is foolproof if thermometer and cook are accurate.

CHRISTMAS FUDGE

3 cups granulated sugar or 3½ cups brown sugar
2 squares unsweetened chocolate
½ cup milk
2 tablespoons butter or margarine
½ cup nuts, chopped
½ cup candied fruit, chopped and cooked in liqueur to soften
1 teaspoon cinnamon

Cook chocolate, 2 cups sugar and milk in double boiler until chocolate is melted and sugar is dissolved. Then add cinnamon and 1 cup of sugar (1½ cups if you use brown sugar). Boil, stirring only to avoid sticking, until mixture begins to thicken (soft ball stage). Remove from heat. Cool to tepid, having added butter. Stir in nuts and candied fruit. Spoon into buttered tin or platter. Sprinkle with red or green sugar, if desired. Cut into squares when hardened.

CRYSTALLIZED GINGER

1 pound fresh ginger roots
1 cup sugar
½ cup water

Clean and peel young ginger roots. Cut into bite-sized pieces. Cover with cold water and soak for at least 1 hour. Drain. Cover once again with cold water, cooking and boiling for 5 minutes. Repeat the draining, covering with cold water and boiling process 3 to 5 times until fruit is tender and transparent. Make a simple syrup of the sugar and water. Boil ginger pieces in syrup for 5 minutes, being sure that pan does not boil dry. Remove ginger pieces from syrup; cool slightly. While still warm, not hot, shake in container filled with granulated sugar. Separate pieces and place on paper towels on a flat surface to dry thoroughly. Store in an air-tight container.

Pickles & Preserves

CHILI SAUCE

Yield: 10 to 12 pints

1 peck (16 pounds) ripe tomatoes
5 large white onions
4 large green peppers
8 cups vinegar
3 tablespoons salt
3 tablespoons celery seed
3 tablespoons white mustard seed
3 tablespoons ground cloves
3 tablespoons allspice
3 tablespoons cinnamon
5 cups sugar

Peel tomatoes. Chop onions and green peppers very fine. Put all ingredients in a large kettle and boil for 3½ hours.

CHUTNEY

Yield: About 2 quarts

1½ pounds or 6 medium ripe tomatoes, chopped
1½ pounds or 6 medium sour apples, chopped
2 quarts cider vinegar
5 lemons, grated rind and juice
½ pound or 1 cup solidly packed brown sugar
1½ pounds or 4½ cups raisins
¼ tablespoons salt
¼ pound or 1 to 2 medium onions, chopped
2 ounces or 4 to 6 cloves garlic, chopped
1 tablespoon curry powder
2 ounces or 10 tablespoons ground ginger
2 ounces or 9 tablespoons dry mustard
½ ounce or 2 tablespoons cayenne pepper
¼ ounce or 1 tablespoon turmeric
¼ ounce or 2 teaspoons white mustard seed

Boil tomatoes, apples and vinegar together until soft. Mash through a colander. Put this mixture and all other ingredients into a kettle and boil ½ hour, stirring constantly. Bottle and seal.

INDIAN MANGO CHUTNEY

Yield: Eight to ten 8-ounce jars

- **1 quart cider vinegar**
- **2 pounds sugar (1 pound can be brown sugar if you like)**
- **8 ripe but firm mangos (9 if they are small), peeled and cut from the seed in small pieces (about ½-inch cubes or smaller)**
- **2 large (or 4 small) regular onions, chopped fine**
- **2 tablespoons commercial pickling spices, tied tightly in *roomy* cheesecloth bag. (The spices expand in cooking and the sugar-vinegar mixture should be able to circulate through the spices, but the spices should not escape into the chutney itself.)**
- **2 large (or 3 small) cloves garlic, peeled and diced finely**
- **1 teaspoon crushed, dried red pepper flakes. (Do not put these in the pickle-spice bag.)**
- **2 cups raisins**
- **2 ounces fresh ginger root (or ½ cup chopped preserved ginger). Fresh ginger root should be peeled and diced finely.**
- **1 small jar pimentos, drained and diced finely (this for color)**
- **1 teaspoon salt**
- **¼ teaspoon ground turmeric**

Combine vinegar, sugar and mangos in a large *enamel* pot until fruit is soft. Add other ingredients and simmer for 30 minutes or longer, stirring often with a wooden spoon, until mixture is thick. Fill sterilized jars with hot mixture and seal immediately. Allow to cool. Clean jars if some of the mixture has spilled over the sides while filling them. Store; refrigeration not necessary unless a jar has been opened.

GRANDMOTHER'S GREEN TOMATO PICKLE

Yield: 16 to 18 jars

1½ pecks (12 quarts) green tomatoes, sliced
12 large onions
1½ cups salt
Cider vinegar
3 pounds dark brown sugar
3 tablespoons white mustard seed
1½ tablespoons celery seed
1½ tablespoons whole cloves
1½ tablespoons whole allspice
3 tablespoons ground mustard
1½ tablespoons ground black pepper
9 small pods hot red pepper (cut up without seeds) or 2 tablespoons dried crushed red peppers

Slice tomatoes and sprinkle with salt. Let stand overnight. Next day wash off salt and drain thoroughly. Cover with good quality cider vinegar and add the remaining ingredients. Boil about 1 hour and put in sterilized jars.

PUMPKIN CHIPS

Yield: 6 jars

1 large ripe pumpkin (6 to 8 pounds)
6 pounds sugar
8 ripe lemons
6 pint size canning jars (be sure air-tight covers fit each jar)

Open top of pumpkin, cutting a large hole so one may remove all the seeds. Cut the seeded pumpkin in 1½ inch strips, do not remove the skin, and cut the strips into a size about 1½ inch square and then slice each square ⅛ inch thick. Place the chips in large cooking pan, alternating with the chips a layer of thinly sliced lemon. (Leave rind on.) Continue the process of layering pumpkin chips and thin slices of the lemon until cooking container is filled to three-fourths its capacity. Pour the 6 pounds of sugar over the contents and let stand overnight. The following morning place the contents over a slow fire. The chips must cook slowly. Watch closely. When they begin to clarify, resembling orange marmalade, remove the contents from the fire. Place the pumpkin chips in the canning jars, cover and seal with the jars' tops. Serve as a preserve.

UNCOOKED CABBAGE PICKLE

Yield: 2 quarts

3⅓ pounds shredded cabbage
1 cup salt
6 onions
3 red hot peppers
1 pound brown sugar
¼ cup horseradish
¼ cup white mustard seed
2 ounces ground mustard
1 teaspoon turmeric
2 teaspoons celery seed
Vinegar

Mix cabbage, onion, salt and peppers and put in bag and let drain overnight. Next day squeeze dry. Add the spices and pack in 2 quart jars or a stone crock. Cover with vinegar.

COOKED CRANBERRY RELISH

Yield: 5 pints

2 quarts cranberries
7 cups sugar
1 pound seedless raisins
2 large oranges, cut up with slivers of peel (no white part)
1 cup vinegar
1 teaspoon cloves
2 teaspoons cinnamon

Place all ingredients in a large pot. Mix and cook over slow fire until cranberries pop and mixture becomes transparent (about 30 minutes). It keeps well and can be frozen.

SPICED GRAPES ANNENCY

Serves 10 to 12

2 to 3 bunches red grapes, seedless preferred
3 cups water
1 cup sugar
7 whole cloves
1 stick cinnamon
¼ lemon
Pinch salt

Wash grapes. Remove stems and seeds, if any, and eliminate any bruised grapes. Put grapes into crocks or jars of your choosing. Make sugar syrup by combining remaining ingredients and boil to soft ball stage (240 degrees). Pour syrup and seasonings over grapes, cover jar and chill for at least 1 day. Will keep several weeks in refrigerator. Serve with your favorite paté, melba toast and a sauterne wine.

MIXED FRUIT MARMALADE

Yield: About eighteen 6 ounce glasses

1 grapefruit
4 oranges
2 lemons
7 cups sugar

Select thin-skinned white grapefruit and yellow oranges if possible rather than the dark russet ones. Peel fruit, discarding white membrane and seeds, saving pulp and juice. Grind peeling in a meat grinder or use food processor. There should be 4 cups of ground peeling, juice and pulp. (If not, add sufficient orange peel, juice and pulp to make up amount needed to get 4 cups.) Cover ground peeling, juice and pulp with 8 cups of water and let stand for 8 to 12 hours. Cook this mixture until the ground peeling is soft. Immediately add sugar. Mix well. Let stand another 8 to 12 hours. Cook the mixture in a large kettle until candy thermometer reaches 220 degrees or the mixture drops heavily from a spoon. Fill scalded jelly jars and seal.

"I am very much obliged to you my dear Fanny for offering to preserve strawberry for me." Martha Washington to her niece, Fanny Bassett Washington, May 24, 1795.

HOT CURRIED FRUIT

Serves 10 to 12

2 tablespoons cornstarch
2 tablespoons sugar
2 to 3 teaspoons curry powder
½ teaspoon ground ginger
½ teaspoon salt
1 (1 pound, 4 ounce) can unsweetened pineapple chunks
1 (1 pound) can peach halves
1 (11 ounce) can Mandarin oranges
Orange juice
1 cinnamon stick
¼ cup (½ stick) butter or margarine
¼ cup brandy
Slivered almonds

In a saucepan combine cornstarch, sugar and spices. Drain and dry fruit. Reserve pineapple juice only and add enough orange juice to equal 2 cups. Stir juice into cornstarch mixture. Cook over low heat, stirring constantly, until thickened and clear. Add cinnamon stick and cook gently for 6 to 8 minutes. Do not boil. In a 2-quart casserole or chafing dish melt butter, add fruit and heat. Add hot curry sauce and heat 4 minutes. To flame at the table, gently warm brandy. Ignite and pour over fruit and serve immediately. Sprinkle with almonds.

WATERMELON RIND PRESERVES

Yield: 3 pints

1 gallon cubed watermelon rind
2 lemons
8 cups sugar

Peel green skin and red portion from white rind of watermelon. Cut rind into ½ inch to 1 inch cubes. Store cubes overnight in lightly salted water in the refrigerator. Cut lemon in half and then thinly slice halves. Combine drained rind, lemon and sugar in large container and cook over medium heat, uncovered, until the rind is translucent and golden in color. Skim foam from the preserves as necessary. Cubes should remain slightly firm and the juice should be very thick and syrupy when cooking is completed.

SWEET PICKLE WATERMELON RIND

Yield: 8 pints

Remove enough rind from a watermelon to yield 7 pounds of fruit. Prepare rind by cutting off green skin and leaving a little of the pink meat. Cut into cubes. Cover with hot water and parboil until rind can be pierced with a toothpick or fork prong. For 7 pounds of fruit make the following syrup:

Syrup

3½ pounds sugar
1 pint vinegar
½ teaspoon oil of cloves
½ teaspoon oil of cinnamon

Drain off water from parboiled fruit. Bring syrup to boiling point and pour over the fruit. Let stand in the kettle or container overnight. Drain the rind. Bring the syrup to boiling point and pour over rind again. Repeat 24 hours later. On the 3rd day heat the rind and syrup and boil a few minutes and put in jars.

SPICED PEACHES

Yield: About 3 quarts

7 pounds peaches, peeled
4 pounds brown sugar
1 quart vinegar
2 ounces cinnamon sticks
1 ounce whole cloves

Put peaches in a stone jar or sterilized glass jar. Boil sugar with vinegar and the spices in linen bags and pour over the peaches. Let stand in a cool place for 4 days. On the 5th day simmer peaches in the vinegar and spices until you can touch the pits with a fork. Skim peaches out, remove pits and boil juice hard for about ½ hour. Pour back into jar, seal and process and they are ready for winter use. Spiced peaches are always better after they have stood for at least 6 weeks. Delicious with hot or cold roast beef.

Libations

Washington's wine cooler.

MULLED CIDER

Serves 6

1 stick cinnamon, 3 inches long
2 whole allspice
2 whole cloves
1 quart cider
⅔ cup brown sugar

Place spices in bag. Boil cider, spices and sugar 5 minutes. Remove spice bag and boil 5 more minutes. Serve hot. *This may be prepared in advance and kept hot over hot water until time for serving.*

REGENT'S ORANGE CORDIAL

Yield: 1 quart

Outer peel of 4 thick-skin oranges
1 quart rye whiskey
1½ pounds granulated sugar

Cut orange peel into small pieces, removing the white part. Put in a ½-gallon glass jar with screw top with 1 quart of good rye whiskey, adding 1½ pounds of granulated sugar. (A good bourbon may be substituted to add to fifth of rye, making the quart.) Shake the tightly closed jar 3 to 5 minutes daily for a month, by which time the sugar will be thoroughly dissolved and the decoction of orange essence well advanced. The longer it stands, the richer the flavor.

EGGNOG

For a small amount—serves 1 to 2:

1 egg, room temperature
1 level tablespoon sugar
¼ cup bourbon whiskey
¼ cup whipping cream
Nutmeg

For a large amount—3 quarts:

1 dozen eggs, room temperature
½ cup sugar
1 fifth bourbon whiskey
1 quart whipping cream
Nutmeg

Break eggs and separate yolks from whites. Beat whites of eggs until stiff. Beat whipping cream until stiff. Beat yolks of eggs to an even consistency, slowly adding sugar. Add whiskey slowly. Fold in beaten egg whites. Fold in whipped cream. Sprinkle with nutmeg.

GRANDMOTHER HARRISON'S EGGNOG

Yield: 1 gallon

1 dozen eggs
12 heaping tablespoons powdered sugar
9 wine glasses good bourbon whiskey
4 wine glasses apple brandy
2 quarts cream

Beat whites and yolks of eggs separately. While beating yolks, stir in powdered sugar. Mix whiskey and brandy and pour slowly (too quickly will cook eggs) over yolks and sugar. Add cream, unwhipped, and finally the stiffly beaten egg whites.

GLOUCESTER JULEP

Liquor
French or apple brandy
Rum
Peach brandy
Sugar
Mint
Strawberries

"A gill of good liquor, good French or Apple brandy and rum in equal parts—say a small wine glass of each, with a dash of good peach brandy to flavour—to a half pint goblet (silver if you have it). Put the sugar in the spirit and let it dissolve and stand until clear. Use little or no water and then fill the goblet with powdered ice and put the sprigs of mint in last without bruising them. Crown with a few strawberries if you have them." *From the collection of Claiborne papers in the possession of the Virginia Historical Society. 1 teaspoon of sugar is the usual amount used.*

MINT BAILEY

2 cups granulated sugar
2 cups very hot (not boiling) water
1 ounce lemon juice
6 stalks mint
2½ ounces gin, rum or vodka

Make a simple syrup by placing 2 cups of sugar in a quart bottle and pouring over it 2 cups of very hot (not boiling) water. Cap and shake until sugar is dissolved. In 10-ounce highball glass, place ½ ounce syrup, 1 ounce lemon juice and crushed mint leaves. Fill glass with crushed ice and add 2½ ounces of gin, rum or vodka. Stir well before serving. Simple syrup keeps well for several days in the refrigerator.

MINT FIZZ SYRUP

Yield: 1 quart

2½ cups water
2 cups sugar
2 large oranges, rind and juice
6 lemons, rind and juice
1 cup chopped mint
Green food coloring, optional

Combine sugar and water in pan and boil 10 minutes. Squeeze oranges and lemons and put juice, rind and mint in bowl. Pour over hot syrup, cover and let stand 2 hours. Strain and cool. Can be stored 2 weeks. To serve, put 3 tablespoons in 8-ounce glass and add soda or ginger ale. Add 1 drop of coloring, if desired. Whiskey can be added.

KIR

Generous twist of lemon
Splash Creme de Cassis
3 to 4 ounces white Bordeaux
3 ice cubes

In a large wine glass, place lemon, Creme de Cassis, white wine and ice cubes. Stir well.

SHERRY FLIP

Serves 4

2 eggs
2 teaspoons powdered sugar
1 pint half and half
4 jiggers dry sherry
Nutmeg

Beat together eggs and sugar with a wire whisk, add half and half and sherry. Pour over cracked ice, shake and strain. Serve in stemmed glasses adding a dash of nutmeg to each.

Engraved "Stiegel" type flip glass.

"THE LINDENS" 18TH CENTURY PUNCH

Serves approximately 12

1 bottle dry white wine
1 bottle champagne
4 ounces brandy

Mix liquors. To serve, pour over a block of molded ice.

ORANGE-LEMON PUNCH

Serves 16

2 cups boiling water
8 teaspoons tea leaves
1½ cups sugar
1 cup lemon juice
5 cups orange juice
2 quarts iced water or ice alone

Pour boiling water over the tea. Steep 5 minutes. Strain. Dissolve sugar in a cup of warm water. Cool. Combine the tea and sugar with remaining ingredients.

PHILADELPHIA FISH HOUSE PUNCH

Serves 16

½ cup superfine sugar
Water
2 quarts light rum, or 1 quart light and 1 quart dark rum
1 quart brandy
¾ cup peach brandy or cordial
2½ cups lemon juice

Mix together sugar and a little water. Add remaining ingredients. Fish House Punch should sit for at least 2 hours before serving.

Mrs. Washington...appeared after a few minutes, welcomed us most graciously and had punch served.

Julian Niemcewicz's Journal, 1798

ICED TEA

Serves 8 to 10

6 tea bags
2 cups boiling water
Juice of 2 lemons (⅓ cup)
1 cup sugar

Steep 6 tea bags in boiling water for 10 minutes. Put lemon juice and sugar in a pitcher and add hot tea. Stir until sugar has dissolved. Add 6 cups of cold water or the equivalent of cold water and ice cubes. Serve the glasses filled with ice and a sprig of mint.

SPICED TEA

Serves 20

6 oranges
6 lemons
18 cups boiling water
2 teaspoons whole cloves
4 teaspoons tea leaves
1 cup pineapple juice
1½ cups sugar

Squeeze juice from oranges and lemons. Pour 6 cups of the boiling water over orange peels and mix in cloves. Cook for 30 minutes. Add tea leaves and let steep for 15 minutes. Strain. Combine the tea mixture with the orange, lemon and pineapple juices and sugar. Stir in the remaining 12 cups of boiling water until sugar is dissolved. May be served hot or iced. Keeps well in the refrigerator.

HOT MULLED WINE

Serves 6 to 8

1 bottle red wine
3 pints water
¼ cup brown sugar
4 teaspoons cinnamon
4 teaspoons allspice
2 teaspoons cloves
6 dashes bitters
Juice of ½ lemon

Combine ingredients. Boil 5 minutes. Serve hot.

DANDELION WINE

Yield: 4 quart bottles

1 gallon dandelion blossoms gathered while the sun is shining so they will be open, over which pour 1 gallon water and let stand in a cool place for 3 days. Then put into a porcelain kettle with the rind of 1 lemon cut fine and also the rind of 3 oranges; boil 15 minutes, then strain. Add the juice of the lemon and oranges and also the pulp with 3 pounds of sugar. When lukewarm, add ½ yeast cake. Let it stand 1 week in a warm place, then strain and let it stand until it stops working, after which bottle.

Washington's silver coffee pot was made by Joseph Anthony of Philadelphia in 1783.

CONTRIBUTORS

Abraham, Dana
Adams, Mrs. Henry
Adams, Mrs. Thomas H.
Addison, Mrs. Joseph
Adler, Mrs. Leopold, II
Alexander, Mrs. Ray, Jr.
Alexander, Mrs. Richard*
Alsop, Mrs. Stewart J.O.
Anderson, Mrs. Thomas D.**
Anderson, Mr. Thomas D.
Anderson, Mrs. W. Leland
Anscheutz, Mrs. Norbert Lee
Atkin, Mrs. Donald R.
Bailey, Mrs. Travis D.
Baldwin, Mrs. John A.
Ball, Mrs. Walter
Banfield, Mrs. Paul Landon
Barclay, Mrs. Albert H., Jr.
Barnes, Mrs. Elmore V.
Bateman, Mrs. Kenneth
Bates, Mrs. Garnetta
Battle, Mrs. Thomas B.*
Beatty, Mrs. Harold A.
Bemis, Mrs. Guy
Bering, Mrs. Edgar A., Jr.
Bishop, Mrs. Clarence M., Jr.*
Blundon, Mrs. Montague
Bockstoce, Mrs. Clifton M.*
Bolton, Mrs. Kenyon C.*
Bonsal, Mrs. Philip W.
Bovaird, Mrs. William
Bowersock, Mrs. Justin D.
Bowman, Mrs. A. Smith
Bradford, Mrs. David*
Brauns, Mrs. Robert
Brewster, Mr. Edward L.
Britton, Mrs. John P.
Brockett, Mrs. Charles L.†
Brooks, Mrs. Michael
Brown, Mrs. Joseph W.
Burdick, Mrs. C. Lalor†
Burke, Mrs. John W., Jr.
Burr, Mrs. Francis H.
Bush, Mrs. George H. W.
Byers, Mrs. Buckley H.
Byrd, Mrs. Richard E.
Carswell, Mrs. Robert
Chisholm, Mrs. Frank A.*
Clay, Mrs. Thomas
Claytor, Mrs. W. Graham, Jr.
Cleveland, Mrs. Donald
Clifford, Mrs. Clark M.
Combs, Mrs. Sydney Sayre
Cook, Mrs. Philip S.
Cooke, Mrs. Thomas Turner*
Cooper, Mrs. John Sherman
Crary, Mary C.
Dalton, Mrs. A. Gerald
D'Amanda, Charlotte Biddle
D'Amanda, Christopher, M.D.
David, Mrs. Sidney
Davidge, Mrs. John Washington, Jr.
Davis, Louise H.
Diers, Mrs. Wallace
Dixon, Mrs. Ben Franklin, III
Dixon, Mrs. W. Frederick
Dodge, Mrs. Clarence, Jr.
Dolega, Mrs. Stanley F.
Eckman, Mary Hynson
Embassy of France
Evans, Mrs. Oliver Marshall
Evans, Mrs. Rowland, Jr.
Falls, Mrs. Bayard T.
Farquhar, Mrs. Norman
Fava, Miss Gloria
Faxon, Frances
Fay, Mrs. Albert Bel
Floyd, Mr. William H.
Frank, Mrs. Randolph Adams
Gaillard, Mrs. David duBose, II
Gilchrist, Mrs. Stewart J.*
Gilliam, Miss Margaret E.
Gillis, Margaret K.
Gray, Mrs. Richmond
Gubser, Mr. Michael
Guy, Mrs. John H., Jr.*

Hagner, Mrs. Randall, Jr.*
Haldeman, Mrs. Walter N.†
Hanks, Mrs. William Vilas*
Harel, Mme. Claude
Harlow, Mrs. John B.
Harrison, Mrs. William B.
Hart, Mrs. Harrie
Hemingway, Mary Moon
Hilliard, Mrs. Thomas J., Jr.
Hillman, Mrs. Henry L.
Holderness, Mrs. George Allen, Jr.
Hollensteiner, Letitia Baldridge
Hollis, Mrs. Daniel W.*
Hooff, Mrs. Charles Rapley, Jr.
Hoskinson, Mr. J. Henry
Howard, Mrs. Nelson A.
Howard, Mrs. Thomas
Hungerpiller, Mrs. James E.
Huxley, Mrs. Matthew
Johnson, Mrs. L. Oakely
Johnson, Mrs. Lyndon Baines
Jones, Mrs. L. Paul
Kassebaum, The Honorable Nancy L.
Kelly, Mrs. W. Bolton
Kelsey, Mrs. Mavis P.
Kitrell, Mrs. Robert
Krech, Mrs. Shepard
Kuhl, Mrs. Nevin E.
Labouisse, Mrs. John W.†
Lane, Mrs. Richard
Lawrence, Mrs. James
Lawrence, Mrs. Sidney
Lewis, Mrs. James C.
Lilly, Mrs. Edward Guerrant, Jr.
Livingstone, Mrs. Ernest T.
Lunt, Mrs. Dudley C.
MacAusland, Mrs. Earl
MacDonald, Mrs. Kenneth
MacIhenny, Mrs. William
Maddux, Mrs. H. Cabell, Jr.
Mann, Mr. William Theodore
Martin, Louise C.
Masterson, Mrs. Harris
Masterson, Mr. Harris
May, Mrs. Ernest Nugent, Jr.
Mayer, Mrs. George J.
McFarland, Mrs. Edward
McMillan, Mrs. James
Metcalf, Mrs. H.P., Jr.
Milch, Mrs. Robert A.
Miles, Mrs. Maud
Miller, Mrs. Allison
Moody, Mrs. Juliette H.
Moore, Mrs. Gene H.
Morrissette, Mrs. H. Taylor*
Neal, Mrs. James T.*
Noel, Mrs. James
Notman, Mrs. Donald D.
Olander, Mrs. Eileen M.*
Olander, Mrs. C.E.
Ongaro, Mrs. Theodore
Pack, Mrs. Arthur N.*
Parrott, Mrs. Thomas A.
Payne, Doris
Peckham, Mr. Rufus Wheeler, Jr.
Pfaelzer, Mrs. David A.*
Pine, Mrs. Whitelaw
Pirtle, Mrs. Alex, Jr.*
Platt, Mrs. Henry Norris†
Rand, Mrs. Ben A.
Reagan, Mrs. Ronald
Redmond, Mrs. J. Woodward
Rice, Mrs. Carew C.*
Risien, Mrs. Raymond S.
Ritchie, Mrs. William L.
Robbins, Mrs. Edward Todd
Roberts, Mrs. Thomas M.
Roseborough, Miss Elizabeth
Ruby, Betty Worster
Russell, Mrs. Thomas J.
Sands, Mrs. Samuel S.
Scarborough, Mrs. William B.
Seamans, Mrs. Robert Channing, Jr.*
Shaw, Mrs. John A.
Sheffield, Mrs. Edwin S.
Smith, Mrs. Henry P., III
Smith, Mrs. Robert Craft
Smith, Mrs. Tom K.*

Snell, Mrs. Burrell D.
Snowdon, Mrs. Henry Taft
Sprunt, Mrs. C. Worth
Standish, Mrs. George A.
Steele, Mrs. Edwin D., Jr.
Steves, Mrs. Marshall
Stinson, Mrs. Tim
Strachan, Mrs. Frank G.*
Streeter, Mrs. Richard H.
Sullivan, Mrs. John L.*
Symington, Mrs. James Wadsworth
Thompson, Mrs. Herbert H.
Todd, Mrs. Augustine Jaquelin*
Turgeon, Mrs. Charlotte
Vanderhoof, Mrs. Richard
Vaughan, Mrs. William L.*
Voorhees, Mrs. John
Wainwright, Mrs. Parsons
Walker, Mrs. Joseph
Walker, Mrs. Peter
Warner, Mrs. Douglas, Jr.
Warner, Mrs. William W.
Waters, Mrs. Joseph F.
Weeks, Mrs. James
Wheeler, Mrs. George Y., III
Wiener, Mrs. Alexander L.*
Wilder, Mrs. Erskine Phelps, Jr.*
Wilder, Lydia
Wiley, Mrs. Robert M.
Williams, Mrs. Douglas*
Willis, Mrs. J. McKenny
Wills, Mrs. Matthew
Winchester, Mrs. George
Wright, Admiral Jerauld

**The Regent, Mount Vernon Ladies' Association, 1984
* Vice Regent, Mount Vernon Ladies' Association
† Former Vice Regent, Mount Vernon Ladies' Association

Index

N

O

P

THE MOUNT VERNON COOKBOOK
Mount Vernon Ladies' Association
Mount Vernon, Virginia 22121

Please send _______ copies of THE MOUNT VERNON COOKBOOK. Enclosed you will find $14.95 per book, plus $3.50 postage and handling per book. Virginia residents add 4.5% sales tax. (Please make checks payable to Mount Vernon Ladies' Association.)

Name ____

Address ____

City ____________________ State ______________ Zip ________

- -

THE MOUNT VERNON COOKBOOK
Mount Vernon Ladies' Association
Mount Vernon, Virginia 22121

Please send _______ copies of THE MOUNT VERNON COOKBOOK. Enclosed you will find $14.95 per book, plus $3.50 postage and handling per book. Virginia residents add 4.5% sales tax. (Please make checks payable to Mount Vernon Ladies' Association.)

Name ____

Address ____

City ____________________ State ______________ Zip ________

- -

THE MOUNT VERNON COOKBOOK
Mount Vernon Ladies' Association
Mount Vernon, Virginia 22121

Please send _______ copies of THE MOUNT VERNON COOKBOOK. Enclosed you will find $14.95 per book, plus $3.50 postage and handling per book. Virginia residents add 4.5% sales tax. (Please make checks payable to Mount Vernon Ladies' Association.)

Name ____

Address ____

City ____________________ State ______________ Zip ________

Reorder Additional Copies

NOTES